Forever Aml
Cray Wanderers F.C. 1860 - 2010
The History of London's Oldest Football Club

by Jerry Dowlen & Peter Goringe
Edited by Mike Floate

Club Honours:

Kent League - 1901-02, 1990-91, 2002-03, 2003-04
Runners Up - 1979/80, 1990/91
Southern Suburban League - 1898/99
West Kent League - 1903/04
London League - 1956/57, 1957/58
Aetolian League - 1962/63
Greater London League - 1965/66
Metropolitan London League - 1974/75
London Spartan League - 1976/77, 1977/78
Ryman League Division One Play Off Winners 2008/09
F.A. Vase Quarter Finalists - 1979/80, 2003/04
Kent Amateur Cup - 1930/31, 1962/63, 1963/64, 1964/65
Kent Senior Trophy - 1992/93, 2003/04
Kent League Cup - 1983/84, 2002/03
London League Cup- 1954/55
Aetolian League Cup- 1963/64
Greater London League Cup - 1964/65, 1965/66
Metropolitan League Cup - 1970/71
Metropolitan League Amateur Shield - 1966/67, 1967/68
Metropolitan London League Cup - 1974/75
Mayor of Uden (Holland) Cup · 1974/75
Sheffield Heritage Tournament Winners - 2010/11

Above: A village event at Fordcroft in the early 1900s.

Designed by Mike Floate
A Football Grounds Frenzy production
Newlands Cottages, 71 Stones Cross Road,
Crockenhill, Swanley, Kent BR8 8LT
© Jerry Dowlen, Peter Goringe, Mike Floate & Cray 150 Publications
ISBN 978-0-9568293-0-6
Printed and bound by F. E. Burman
Crimscott Street, London SE1 5TF 020 7206 1000

Cray Wanderers FC: 150 Years 1860 to 2010
A Welcome from Gary Hillman (Chairman)

It gives me great pleasure to see in print this History Book of Cray Wanderers Football Club, telling the club's story from 1860 to the present day.

150 years is a massive landmark for a football club to reach - the more so when we reflect that Cray Wanderers is the second oldest football club in the world.

Cray Wanderers are very much on a "high" at the moment. The first team is playing in the Ryman Premier League. This is the highest level of football at which the club has ever played.

We also have a thriving reserve team, a newly-formed (2009) young academy team in partnership with Coopers Technology College, and junior teams for all ages under-eights to under-eighteens inclusive.

This demonstrates a big commitment by Cray Wanderers to "grass roots" football in the borough, and to provide playing and coaching resources to all who want to enjoy and succeed at playing the game.

Cray Wanderers has proved that it can provide a pathway for young players to progress all the way to the top in football. During the last ten years, two players who began playing as juniors for the Wands have secured full-time professional contracts with Football League clubs. Sam Wood is a first team regular at Brentford, and young George Porter (age 17) has just made his first team debut for Leyton Orient. Last year, George started playing for the Cray Wanderers academy team and immediately went into the Cray first team, scoring 11 goals for the club in the Ryman Premier League.

Celebrating our 150th anniversary

To make the year 2010 extra special for Cray Wanderers, we have staged a number of successful and diverse events.

Our charity ball was attended by 350 people. I am delighted that a most enjoyable evening spent among friends old and new, saw us raise more than £15,000 for the Bromley Y local youth charity.

An exhibition of Cray Wanderers 150 years history was staged at the London Borough of Bromley Museum during May and June. It was featured on the GMTV London news programme on 22 May.

Our 2010-11 playing season started with a special invitation match against our traditional old local rivals Crockenhill FC. We played the match at St Mary Cray Recreation Ground, near to where the Cray Wanderers used to play in Victorian times.

Two notable "firsts" in the history of Cray Wanderers occurred when we played against a full Football League team (Leyton Orient) in July for the first ever time in the club's history, and then in August came an even more remarkable first-ever occasion, a match against a full international team (Guyana).

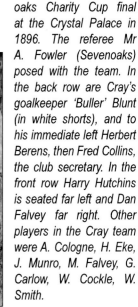

Left: Before the Sevenoaks Charity Cup final at the Crystal Palace in 1896. The referee Mr A. Fowler (Sevenoaks) posed with the team. In the back row are Cray's goalkeeper 'Buller' Blunt (in white shorts), and to his immediate left Herbert Berens, then Fred Collins, the club secretary. In the front row Harry Hutchins is seated far left and Dan Falvey far right. Other players in the Cray team were A. Cologne, H. Eke, J. Munro, M. Falvey, G. Carlow, W. Cockle, W. Smith.

Cray Wanderers FC
1860 -2010

The Future

Celebrating the past history of Cray Wanderers is all well and good, but it counts for nothing if the club cannot be assured of its future.

The name "Wanderers" has proved to be a prophetic one for the club. Never in its 150 years of existence has the club owned its own permanent ground.

Worse still, since the loss of the Grassmeade ground in St Mary Cray in 1973, the Wands have been in exile outside the Crays. The club has been headquartered at Oxford Road in Sidcup, with the first team playing its home matches at Bromley F.C. since 1998.

That is why I have announced a mission statement: "Football's Coming Home!" We want to bring Cray Wanderers back to its homeland in the Crays, and to establish our own permanent home there. We have started a project to build by 2014 a new eco-friendly 5,000-seater stadium at Sandy Lane in St Pauls Cray.

I am encouraged by the many messages of support that have come to us. The big turn-out of local support at St Mary Cray Recreation Ground for our match against Crockenhill on 3 July was very heartening. It showed that Cray Wanderers still belongs to the Crays.

In non-league football it is about the community spirit, pride, tradition, and not just money like higher up the football pyramid. With the knock-on effect of the disappointing 2010 World Cup, more and more people are turning their backs on the professional game. Hopefully we can capitalise on that and get people interested in Cray Wanderers.

Thank You

I would like to take this opportunity to thank everyone who has played a role at Cray Wanderers F.C. over the years. As the pages of this History Book will show, the club's continuing existence has depended upon the commitment of many dedicated individuals who have kept the Wands going through good times and bad.

The club has come a long way in 150 years. Just one more big push from all of us, and the club can achieve what is arguably the most important objective of all – to secure its own permanent home.

Here's to the next 150 years.

Come on you Wands!

Gary Hillman
November 2010

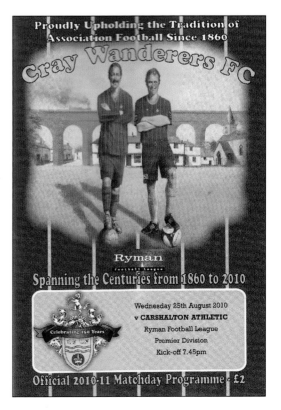

The origins of Cray Wanderers

Founded in 1860, Cray Wanderers is the second-oldest football club in the world. Only Sheffield F.C., which started life three years earlier, claims an earlier foundation date. Although much of the early history of the club, and indeed all football in north-west Kent is shrouded in mystery, there is plenty of strong evidence that football began to be played in the Crays, in a reasonably organised way, 150 years ago. Despite many ups and downs, frequent crises and more than one occasion when the club was on the point of extinction, we can trace a continuous thread from 1860 to the successful and ambitious Cray Wanderers F.C. of today.

Football in various forms has been played on the fields of England for many centuries, but it was only in Victorian times that the first attempts were made to provide any regulation or organisation of the sport. The Football Association was founded in 1863; one of its first tasks was to come to some agreement over the rules of the game, as there were many local variations. The F.A. Cup started nine years later.

These developments, though, had little impact at first on the playing of football in the Crays. The Victorian pioneers of organised football were gentlemen, from the universities and old boys of the public schools. The origins of Cray Wanderers lay in an altogether different walk of life.

The tale actually begins not in 1860, but at a club meeting in 1905. A dispute arose during this meeting over the date of the club's foundation. George Wheeler related how he and other young men started the team in 1860 and called themselves the Cray Wanderers. They played their matches on a recreation ground, which is now the site of the Star Lane cemetery, adjacent to the railway line in St Mary Cray (this site was previously known as Tyrersfield). As George put it, 'It didn't matter much whether it was a long or round ball'.

It was the building of the railway that holds the key to the foundation of Cray Wanderers. From 1858 the East Kent Railway started building a line from Rochester to the coast. In order to gain access to London, it needed to link up with the Mid-Kent railway, which at that time ran as far as Bickley. So, between 1858 and 1860, the London, Chatham and Dover Railway (as it became known in 1859) constructed the missing link between Rochester and Bickley.

This required the line to cross the Cray Valley. Huge embankments had to built almost entirely by manual labour. Hundreds of labourers from outside the Crays (including Irish workers) literally camped in the area. They completed the nine-arch red brick viaduct that carries the line over St Mary Cray High Street in December 1860. In their leisure time, the labourers would kick a football around. Eventually some of these men and locals started a football team. George Wheeler (who, according to the census, was 20 years old in 1860 and lived at 73, St Mary Cray High Street) explained that matches were played against army and other village sides.

The name of the team, Wanderers, was one that was often used for sides that included players from outside the local area, so this is consistent with the migrant workers helping to establish the club. However, there is another story that was relayed by club stalwart, Ernie Harman: 'The same story was given to me by three elderly gentlemen at different times, and it was that one day at the end of a game Arthur (Bowser) Price was asked, 'What did you think of us?' His reply was, 'You looked like a bunch of Wanderers.' At the next meeting this was mentioned and from then on it was Cray Wanderers.'

The footballers used Barnard's Coffee Tavern, a listed building that still stands in St Mary Cray High Street (numbers 7 to 9). From here the footballers would have walked by the Old Star public house on the corner of Star Lane, past the old cottages, to take the field at the Star Lane pitch.

The sport during these early days would seem, from the perspective of the 21st century, to have been somewhat haphazard. It is believed that hundreds of clubs came into existence all over the country during the 1860s and 1870s but there was considerable reluctance to join either the F.A. or the Rugby Union. In fact, affiliated clubs were in a minority until the early 1880s, when the Kent F.A. was formed. Indeed, along-

**Cray Wanderers FC
1860 -2010**

Founded 1860

Cray Wanderers FC 1860 -2010

Founded 1860

side inter-village matches, it is likely that often football clubs were an arrangement between members to meet weekly in a local farmers field and choose teams amongst themselves. (Beards v Cleanshaven, Married v Unmarried etc). The exact type of football played would depend on who brought which shape of ball, and the local rules. Because of their casual nature and because they lay outside the jurisdiction of the governing bodies they remained largely unreported by the press.

It is likely that many of the earliest games would have been a form of rugby, but soccer grew in popularity through the 1870s. Ernie Harman was told the story of the time when a game was arranged with the Swifts from Sidcup. When they came on to the field it was seen that Cray had 15 players against 11 of the visitors, who were a soccer side. So Cray took four players off and enjoyed the game very much!

Bert Booker, whose family have been connected with Cray Wanderers for generations, vividly remembers two team photos that his grandfather hung on either side of the hearth. These were of the last Cray Wanderers rugby team, and the first Cray Wanderers soccer team. The photos were said to have been taken on the same day. Based on the names of some of players that Bert was told were in the photos, it may have been as late as the mid-1880s that the Wanderers finally became an Association Football Club.

Right: A newspaper report for a 3-1 win for Cray Wanderers on 20 October 1888.

Certainly, the first press reports of matches involving Cray Wanderers are a little confusing. In December 1886 it was reported that St Mary Cray defeated St John's Institute by a goal to nil. Most of the players listed appeared for Cray Wanderers in subsequent years. The following month the Bromley Telegraph reported that Cray Wanderers had lost to Hawks (Bromley) by a goal kicked by J. Payne from a try obtained by A. Freeman, to nil. The report of the same match in the Sidcup Times refers to a goal coming from a corner by J. Payne. Rugby or soccer? Maybe the reporters were not entirely sure!

By this time, Cray Wanderers were playing home matches at the Recreation Ground, also known as Derry Downs at Grigg's Cross. This may well be the same piece of land as the current recreation ground but could have been the field that became Grassmeade.

There are a couple of reports of games in the 1887-88 season, including a 2-2 draw with Southall. Without doubt these were games of soccer. By the 1888-9 season, Cray's second as a pure Association Football club, reporting of both forms of football in the press became much more thorough and a full account of the matches of Cray Wanderers can be found.

The first game of this season must have been something of a shock, as Millwall Rovers won 8-0 at St Mary Cray. The visitors were the predecessors of Millwall F.C. and competed in much more exalted circles for the rest of the season; they played the likes of Tottenham Hotspur and entered the F.A. Cup. Cray, meanwhile, played more local opponents, including the predecessors of Dartford and Erith. In the away games against both these teams, the Wanderers lost in controversial circumstances. Dartford's winner in their 4-3 victory was apparently aided by spectators getting in the way of Cray's players, whilst Erith's winning goal was also disputed. In reference to the scorer, the local paper commented, 'Some discussion arose as to his being offside'. Over the years there have been many such discussions!

The transformation of the Wanderers from one of countless casually-organised village sides to a prominent local football side was due to two men: Herbert Berens and Harry Hutchins.

CRAY WANDERERS v. CRAYFORD YOUNG MEN'S FRIENDLY SOCIETY.

This Association match was played on Saturday, October 20th, when the Cray team visited Crayford, being conveyed there in a pair-horse brake (supplied by Messrs. W. A. Dowling, of Sidcup), and a very pleasant day was spent. Play commenced soon after three, Crayford having the pick of goals. The game was rather slow the first half, the ball being kept well in the vicinity of the home team's goal. Soon, however, Dashwood, assisted by R. Sharp and G. Smith, succeeded in obtaining the first goal for the visitors. The ball being again in play the visitors once more had the best of it, this time J. Allen obtaining the goal. After half-time the home team made a determined stand, but were unsuccessful in preventing H. Hutchings from placing the ball between their posts. Crayford then pulled themselves together and the play was very fast and in the visitor's territory, several good kicks at goal being made but were repelled by J. Bassett (goal). Soon, however, McGregor, from a pass by R. Wilkins, sent the ball, after hitting the cross bar, through the Wanderers' goal. No other points were gained by either side, the Cray Wanderers being the victors by three goals to one.

The following composed the teams:—Crayford: W. Dartnell, goal; R. G. Hewitt, H. Phillips, backs; R. Fooks, F. Brown, E. Hewitt, half-backs; G. Pilling, McGregor, H. Webb, W. Axtell, and R. Wilkins (centre), forwards. Cray Wanderers: J. Bassett (goal), W. Hawes, A. Palmer, backs; J. Palmer, E. Packman, G. Smith, half-backs; H. Dashwood, R. Sharp, J. Allen, W. Packman, and H. Hutchings (centre), forwards.

**Cray Wanderers FC
1860 -2010**

Berens was the son of the area's largest land-owner, Richard Berens, who owned Kevington Manor. He was educated at Westminster School and returned to the Crays to manage his father's estate. He was also captain of the Cray Valley District Fire Brigade. An excellent footballer, he played for the Wanderers from around 1889 to 1896. But of more significance than his great playing ability was the financial and organisational support Berens and his family provided for the club.

Hutchins was a very popular local man. An undertaker by profession, he previously played for Southall, who in 1887 won the West Middlesex Cup. A prolific goalscorer, he was instrumental in the rise of Cray Wanderers from 1888 to the end of the century. He was captain of the club and, playing at centre-forward, was adored by supporters for his football skills and sharp tactical brain. If all the goals he scored had been recorded by the press, he would probably be second to Ken Collishaw in the club's all time list.

The beginning of competitive football

Cray Wanderers took a big step forward in 1889 when they entered their first competition – the Kent Junior Cup. The first round took them to Westerham. The Wanderers travelled by train and were surprised not to be met at the sta-tion, or to have been provided with any dressing rooms! Putting these setbacks aside, Cray comfortably won their first competitive match 4-1, with Hutchins, Harry Dashwood and Bob Sharp amongst the goals.

The next round brought the Northumberland Fusiliers to St Mary Cray, albeit three quarters of an hour late. Hutchins scored a hat-trick as Cray won 4-3. The end of Cray's first cup run came in the next round, the quarter-final, when Royal Arsenal Reserves won 2-0.

Later in the season, there was an unpleasant incident at Dartford. The home side, having taken the lead, kept on deliberately kicking the ball off the pitch, a practice known at the time as fluking. This was considered to be highly unsporting and, having given his opposite number a warning that went unheeded, Hutchins led his Cray team off and the match was abandoned.

Cray had an even better run in the Kent Junior Cup the following season. They reached the semi-final, before losing narrowly to the eventual winners, Royal Artillery (Sheerness). In 1891-92 the Wanderers finally reached the final, having beaten Chatham Reserves 3-2 in the semi-final at Maidstone. The long trip to Folkestone was a big disadvantage and Cray had to be content with the runners-up medals, after losing a

Left: The Cray Wanderers team for the Kent Junior Cup semi-final versus Royal Artillery in 1891. Harry Hutchins (centre forward and captain) is seated in the middle of the front row, with Herbert Berens to his right. The committee men are believed to be Mr Ellis and Mr Greenslade. In the back row, the player third from left is Jimmy Hutton. Other players probably in the photo are Harry Dashwood, Tom Hancock, Nat Mercer, Bob Sharp, H.C. Sharp and George Smith.

Cray Wanderers FC
1860 -2010

Founded 1860

closely-fought contest 3-2 to the Highland Light Infantry Reserves.

This same season saw the Wanderers honoured with an invitation to play in the Chatham Charity Cup, a sure sign of growing repute. A 6-2 defeat of the Royal Marines put Cray into the semi-final, but Chatham crushed them 7-0. In the same week Chatham, who were F.A. Cup quarter-finalists a couple of weeks earlier, were themselves beaten 5-0 by Everton! A well-known player for Cray at this time was Arthur Christmas, who had played for Arsenal's first-team in the F.A. Cup, against Derby County.

The Wanderers made the step up to the Kent Senior Cup in 1892, losing to Erith 3-1 at home, following a 1-1 draw. There were some excellent results in friendly matches, including a fine 2-1 win at Ashford, a commendable 2-1 defeat at the Royal Engineers, as well as 11-1 and 7-0 victories over the newly-formed Bromley F.C.

Cray had some difficulty in arranging friendly fixtures against teams of a suitable standard. They only needed 10 players to beat Sidcup F.C. 16-1, the club's record victory in any match. In three consecutive games in October, the Wanderers scored 32 goals!

The 1892-3 season saw Cray's first two players to be capped for Kent. Bob Sharp, a half-back

Right: Jack Graham from Sidcup played for the Wands in 1892 and went on to be Millwall's star defender, later moving on to Woolwich Arsenal and Brentford. The old cry 'keep it on the island' has been attributed to Jack when playing for Millwall at East Ferry Road, Isle of Dogs, for it was his long kicking which was the inspiration for the expression.

who had been playing for the club since 1886, received great praise for his performance against Surrey in December. Right-back Jack Graham played twice for Kent, before being snapped up by Millwall. He captained their side, which won the first two Southern League titles and took on the likes of Liverpool and Wolves in the F.A. Cup, and was a well-known professional player.

After avenging the Erith defeat (3-2 after extra time), Cray found themselves not only in the Chatham Cup semi-final but in the position of being favourites to beat Sheppey and go on to take the trophy. But the Wanderers lost 2-1 and Sheppey emphatically defeated Ashford 4-1 in the final.

1893-4 brought another first, as Cray participated in the inaugural F.A. Amateur Cup, beating Erith 2-0 in the first qualifying round before falling 3-0 to Royal Ordnance in the next. The fixture list was considerably strengthened, but the diet of friendly matches brought its own problems. In fact, in November the Wanderers found themselves facing a team of almost Football League quality, when they travelled to Woolwich expecting to play Arsenal's Athletic XI (Reserves). They got caught up in a convoluted dispute between Royal Ordnance and Arsenal Athletic as to the relative strength of their teams and were on the receiving end of an 8-0 defeat.

A week later, Cray made the long trip to Folkestone and lost 6-2. The seasiders complained about the weak side the Wanderers had brought, which drew an indignant reply from Cray's indefatigable secretary, Fred Collins. He explained how difficult it was to organise a strong team for such a long journey on a Saturday, which for many men was still part of the working week.

In March Cray's reputation was restored when they drew 1-1 at New Brompton and might have won. New Brompton, who later became Gillingham, were second only to Arsenal in Kent Football at this time. They claimed to have fielded a weakened side, but Cray could point out that nine men who had been capped for Kent were in their team.

League Football begins

No doubt the difficulties and disputes caused by friendly fixtures were amongst the reasons why the first league football in the county got underway in 1894. Cray were placed in the second division of the Kent League. At this time, the Kent F.A. formally allowed professionalism, and it appears that some of Cray's players were paid, as the club did not compete in the F.A. or Kent Amateur Cup again until 1907. There may have been an agreement with Arsenal, whereby the Wanderers gave competitive football to what might now be termed fringe players, but it is unlikely that this was a formal nursery club arrangement.

The first Kent League game was a 2-1 defeat at Chatham A, but Cray soon found their feet. 900 spectators were at the Rec. to see the first home league victory (3-1 v Faversham) and in November Sevenoaks were defeated to the tune of 15-0, which remains Cray's record score in any competitive match.

As the season progressed, though, problems began to emerge. The committee all but disbanded and it was only due to the sterling efforts of Herbert Berens and Harry Hutchins that the club was kept on an even keel. The new professionals proved fickle and from February, Cray's reserve side, made up of local youngsters, effectively took over the first team's fixtures. They became known as The Berens Boys and did just as well as the outsiders, finishing third in the league.

For the 1895-96 season, the famous colours of amber and black were first adopted by the club. Third place was again reached in the league, but the highlight of the season was a place in the final of the Sevenoaks Charity Trophy. The Wanderers were privileged to play at the Crystal Palace, then the home of the F.A. Cup final; this was the Victorian equivalent of playing at Wembley. 400 supporters made the trip but alas, as so often during this period, Sheppey would provide an insurmountable obstacle, as they won 1-0. Cray Reserves brought success to the club, winning the Sevenoaks Charity Cup (then a league competition), a trophy still competed for today. They also stood in for the first team in a Kent League promotion test match, which clashed with the final at Crystal Palace. Not surprisingly,

the Reserves lost (6-0 to Swanscombe) but the Wanderers had the last laugh as, due to resignations, they were promoted to the Kent League first division anyway.

In 1897, Cray decided to enter a second league, the South Suburban, to supplement their fixtures in the Kent League. They made a good start in both leagues, but suffered a terrible blow in early December when the death of Herbert Berens was announced, due to pneumonia and acute bronchitis. Aged just 30, he was club treasurer and captain of the Reserves. A huge crowd attended his funeral, with Fred Collins and captain Harry Eke representing Cray Wanderers and Harry Hutchins the Fire Brigade.

Right: The Sevenoaks Charity Cup.

Below: Cray's Reserve team with the Sevenoaks Charity Cup, 1895-96.

CRAY WANDERERS TEAM 1895-96.

Cray Wanderers FC 1860 -2010

Founded 1860

In an anonymous tribute published in 1932, the author wrote, 'If ever there was a man of whom it could be said he did good by stealth it was the one time captain of the Wanderers. No-one will ever know quite all that he (and his family) did for the old club, and no-one could measure the joy that he derived from his games with Wanderers.'

Cray's form declined sharply for the rest of the season, but Berens left the club an important legacy. Shortly before his death, he had been working to find the club a new and permanent ground. The Recreation Ground at Derry Downs was open land, owned by Mr E.H. Joynson, whose St Mary Cray Paper Mill provided the Bank of England with the paper for the first £1 notes. Mr Joynson would only allow admission charges to be taken on Boxing Day and Easter Monday, but the locals refused to pay anyway! Thanks to Herbert Berens' negotiations, Joynson offered the Wanderers a piece of land at Fordcroft (on Cray Avenue, where the Tip Top factory later stood). The rent was very small and the ground could be fully enclosed so that admission could be charged at all games. Mr Joynson also conveyed the grandstand from the Recreation Ground on one of his vehicles. It was dismantled and rebuilt at the new ground.

Success at Fordcroft

Whether it was the simply the income from admission charges, or further sponsorship from Mr Joynson, we will never know, but Cray's first few years at Fordcroft were enormously successful. In their first season at the ground, the South Suburban League title was won in style, with just one defeat. This was the first step towards the great sides of the early 1900s, built around G. Flower in goal and full-backs Jack Rogers and Sack Taylor. Half-backs such as Harry Eke and Lionel Jordan were the engine-houses of the team, whilst wingers Dan Falvey and Kibble Highwood produced crosses for Jack Moody, another voracious centre-forward, who arrived from Arsenal in 1899.

However, tragedy struck Fordcroft before the ground had been in use for two years. On Easter Monday 1900, during a reserve team match, lightning struck the grandstand. Charles Davies, a sailor who was watching the match, was killed. There were many injuries amongst the spectators and players, including Sack Taylor, George Wheeler and Fred Brigden, who recalled the incident in 1950: 'Although I wasn't playing that day, I went to the dressing room with my friends in the team. Something like a hammer seemed to hit me at the back of the head … and many others were so dazed after the incident that we walked in opposite directions to our homes. For years afterwards many people had marks in the shape of trees on their arms and legs.'

It was the 1900-01 season that first brought the Wanderers to countywide prominence, as they reached the final of the prestigious Kent Senior Cup.

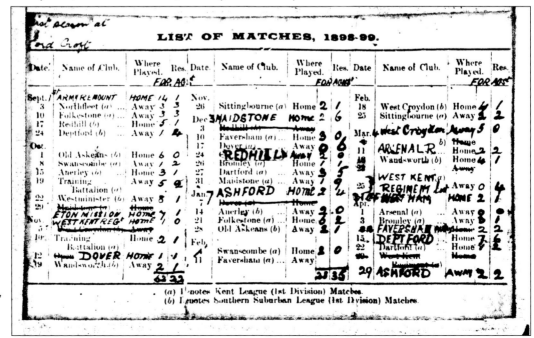

**Right**: Fixture card 1898-99. Note the words 'First Season at Fordcroft' handwritten in the top corner.

After defeating Bromley and 3rd Kent Artillery, Cray overcame Sittingbourne in quarter-final at Fordcroft, with Moody and Newbold scoring, and then beat Chatham 3-0 in the semi-final at Bromley. The final was played in torrential rain at Chatham and Kent League champions Maidstone United soon took a three-goal lead. This was the final score.

Cray's side was strengthened still further for the following campaign. Amongst the acquisitions was Robert Turner, who had previously played for Newton Heath in the Football League Division Two. Newton Heath were re-named Manchester United in 1902. Turner was one of a number of what might be called journeyman professionals who had spells with Cray during the early years of the 20th Century. After leaving Manchester in 1899, he played for Southern League Brighton United. One can only assume that there was a financial incentive for a player of this calibre to come to play at a little-known village side in the Kent League. It may have been another example of Mr Joynson's generosity or perhaps the Arsenal connection had something to do with it.

A 5-0 defeat at Folkestone in the first game of the 1901-02 season did not suggest that Cray were going to challenge for the Kent League title, but this was followed by a succession of high-scoring wins that took the Wanderers to the top of the table, neck and neck with Sittingbourne. The sides finished with equal points, which, according to the rules, required a play-off to decide the title. This took place on 25th April at Chatham's ground and Moody scored the only goal during extra-time. This was a tremendous achievement for Cray, as the status of the Kent League was very high before the First World War.

Cray almost pulled off a remarkable double, as in the West Kent League (which they had entered for the first time) they were runners-up by a single point to Arsenal Reserves. They repeated this performance the following season, but finished well down the Kent League. A significant event in October 1902 was Cray's first appearance in the F.A. Cup, another sign of the growing confidence of the club. Deptford Town were overcome 2-1 on their own ground in the Preliminary Round, followed by defeat at Maidstone by the same scoreline.

1903-04 saw Cray move exclusively to the West Kent League, which was challenging the supremacy of the older league. There was a change of goalkeeper as Flower left the club. One press report wrote of him: The 'Flower' that bloomed in the Wanderers' goal was a very hardy plant indeed, and used his hands and feet with ability

Left: Cray Wanderers 1899-1900. Back row (L to R) Kibble Highwood, G Flower, Jack Rogers, Sack Taylor, T Christmas. Middle row: L Ogburn, J Moody, P Robertson, F Newbold. Front row: E Cooper, B Phillips, Lionel Jordan. Can you spot the player whose shirt has the initials 'CW' sewn on?

Cray Wanderers FC 1860 -2010

Founded 1860

Right: Tommy Wilcox was Cray's goalkeeper in 1902-03 and 1903-04. He later played in the Football League for Blackpool (a whole season 1905-06) and Manchester United (two first-team appearances in 1908-09).

Below: Kent League champions 1901-02.

and judgement.

He also received fulsome praise in a tribute to the Cray team of the turn of the century, which was printed in the *Kentish Times* some 30 years later,

There was Flower, the goalkeeper. Ah, you young footballers of today – what a fine example of a goalkeeper for you. His modesty, his quiet humour, his deadly earnestness when faced with a hot attack, his utter fearlessness in a melee, and his characteristic return to his charge after clearing, tugging with both hands at the peak of his cap. I can hear the cheers and shouts of 'Good old Flower!' and I can see his admirable demeanour in the dressing room afterwards when the congratulations of his fellows were being showered on him. Yes, Flower was a very popular man in the Wanderers team of that day.

Flower's replacement was Tommy Wilcox, who joined from Arsenal's reserve side. He was a very interesting character, who was born at sea and was world champion at the sport of punch-ball – apparently a gymnastic routine involving the equipment used for training boxers. Wilcox proved to be just as much a star as Flower. A true wanderer, after two years with Cray he was signed by Norwich City, then in the Southern League, before playing for Manchester United (two appearances) and Blackpool in the Football League. His later career took him to Carlisle, Goole (near Hull) and Abergavenny in Wales!

Harold Lee was another signing, who alongside Moody and an exciting new winger, A.J. Hawkins, scored most of the goals in 1903-04. A teenager from Erith, Lee moved on to Sittingbourne at the end of the season, before transferring to Arsenal.

Like Wilcox, he also played professionally in the north-west, making 50 appearances for Bury in the Football League First Division.

It is remarkable that these highly-talented players were turning out for Cray in the West Kent League. The Wanderers duly won the title, by eight points from their nearest challengers, the short-lived Eltham F.C. In the Kent Senior Cup, though, it was Eltham who took the plaudits. Cray's 1-0 victory over Kent League leaders Chatham in the quarter-final was regarded as a shock by the mid-Kent press, but they had to acknowledge West Kent's superiority when Eltham beat Sittingbourne comfortably in the final, having defeated the Wanderers 1-0 in a very close semi-final at Gravesend.

A shadow of their former self

Sadly, this second famous championship marked a high point in the club's fortunes. The 1904-05 was a reasonably good one, with third place in the league and narrow defeats to Eltham and Sittingbourne in the F.A. and Kent Senior Cups. After that, however, Cray were not the same force for over 20 years.

A number of factors seem to have contributed to this. By the start of the 1905-06 season, all of the 'journeymen' had moved on; Hawkins

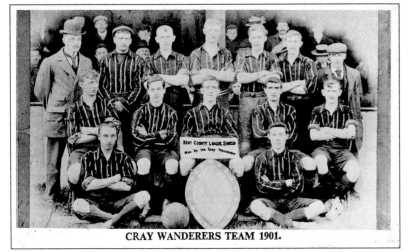

CRAY WANDERERS TEAM 1901.

was snapped up, almost inevitably, by Arsenal. Presumably the backing that had allowed Cray to attract players of that pedigree was dried up. The remarkable Fred Collins stepped down after serving as Hon. Secretary for 14 years and several local players came to the end of their illustrious careers. And, to make matters worse, strong new rivals appeared on the scene, to challenge Cray's position as leading club in the area.

New Crusaders, formed by the Headmaster of Sidcup College, Samuel Farnfield, primarily for the benefit of his six footballing sons, immediately started to play at the highest levels of the amateur game. They reached the first round proper of the F.A. Cup in 1905 and entertained Plymouth Argyle. News of their exploits soon came to dominate the sports pages of the local press, at the expense of details about the Wanderers.

A closer rival was Orpington F.C., who played behind the White Hart public house. Cray had opposed their election to the West Kent League in 1904, but The Cockerels were able to take up their place 12 months later. A 3-1 victory for Cray in this local derby, before nearly 2,000 spectators on Boxing Day, was a morale booster, but Orpington had the last laugh, finishing runners-up, one place above the Wanderers. Eltham were the league champions with a 100% record and also won the Kent Senior Cup.

But all of this paled into insignificance when the people of St Mary Cray were dealt a crushing blow on 12th July 1906. A party of local tradesmen and fire-fighters hired a double-deck Vanguard omnibus for a day's excursion to Brighton. It appears that the brakes failed as the vehicle was descending the notorious Handcross Hill, south of Crawley. Ten men were killed and 26 were injured in what remains the worst road accident in Sussex history. An inquest put much of the blame on the construction of the city bus which was unsuitable for country roads.

Amongst the dead was Harry Hutchins. He had retired from playing about six years earlier, having led Cray Reserves to the Bromley & District League championship in 1899-1900, but he remained a key figure at the club. There was a mass funeral ten days later and the men were buried in St Mary Cray cemetery. An old sup-

porter paid this tribute to Hutchins, 'I believe the team would have died for Harry. Apart from the fine game he played –crafty, bustling, sure and entirely unselfish – he had that great gift of inspiring in others the doggedness that knows not defeat till the whistle goes for 'time.' Many an apparent lost game have I seen turned into victory by the superhuman efforts and unquenchable optimism of the Wanderers' skipper. No wonder his team loved him! His smile disarmed them. Of all those who mourned his tragic and untimely death in the terrible disaster as Handcross, none could have been more sincere than his old colleagues at the Cray Wanderers Football Club.'

No wonder that the 1906-07 commenced under a cloud. The *Kentish Times* described the club as a shadow of their former self and wrote of the disarray into which they had fallen. There was even concern that the club might go to the wall. It was decided to re-enter the Kent League, whilst remaining in the West Kent League. Results were moderate, but most of the home games were won, which raised spirits of the supporters. Cray played New Crusaders in an end-of-season friendly and did not disgrace themselves in a 2-4 defeat.

Left: A strong Cray team indeed. Wilcox and Moody were ex-Arsenal players. Hawkins went on to sign for Arsenal.

BROMLEY v. CRAY WANDERERS.

WEST KENT LEAGUE.

The local rivalry existing between these two clubs usually secures a large attendance whenever they meet, and it is rarely that more than a goal separates them at the finish of their matches, but on Saturday, when they met for the second time this season, the Wanderers easily asserted their superiority and won handsomely 5—1. Bromley were not at full strength, and Cray were one short of their League eleven, and the general opinion on the ground was that the game would be a close one. The band of St. Joseph's Home, Orpington, agreeably whiled away the time till a start was made. Bromley won the toss, but there was not much to be gained by it, and Cray started the game. At the outset the visitors had much the best of the play, and two or three fine centres were got in that placed the Wanderers' goal in peril, but there was a sad want of following up by the inside men, with the result that the Cray backs cleared with freedom. In one of these clearances the Cray forward string got on the march, and Lee, shooting the ball out to Hawkins, the Cray wing man soon had the Bromley defence in difficulties. Hawkins shot for goal, Soppitt gathering the ball with his feet, and Lee and Moody promptly closed in on him. The ball was ultimately got away by Soppitt, but it went to Hawkins, who this time centred across the goal, and although Lee missed it Highwood was at hand, and the first goal was registered with ease. Quickly following on this success the Cray front string wove their way to Ashworth again, and a corner resulted. This Highwood was entrusted with, and the ball was dropped in the middle of the entrance to goal where Moody met it with his head, and it fell over Ashworth's back into goal, the sun apparently, which was streaming in his eyes, preventing Ashworth from seeing the real position of affairs. A free kick against Taylor just outside the penalty line should have given Bromley a chance, but Devine, with a fine opening, shot wide. A penalty against Bromley was the next incident, Soppitt charging Lee from behind, and Hawkins made the best of his opportunity by placing the third goal to the Wanderers' account. Highwood was working well, and two of his centres went astray, but from a tall pass Hawkins had a race in open country and placed in front of goal brilliantly. Lee lost it, but Everist was close at hand and banged the ball into goal, Ashworth not shaping for it.

Hudd got clean away and sent the ball well forward, and then raced Rogers for it. Wilcox, however, judged the distance and ran forward and reached it first. The interval shortly after was signalled, when Cray were leading 4—0. Bromley opened the second part in promising style and swarmed around Wilcox, who twice in a very few minutes had to use his hands, and he was lucky to get rid of a shot from Stapley by putting his foot out and booting it. But presently the Wanderers came again, and from a centre by Highwood the ball fell at the feet of Hawkins, who scored the fifth point without moving a step. A few long shots were then tried by the Cray halves, but none had any effect, but from a rebound off one of the Bromley defenders Hawkins was left with only Ashworth to upset. The shot went high and Ashworth tipped it over the bar—one of his finest strokes of the afternoon—and from the corner he again cleverly got the ball from his goal. A splendid run was then made by Stapley, Taylor kicking out to frustrate him, but Noall getting the ball let drive with the best shot of the day that came from Bromley. Wilcox caught the ball in his arms but dropped it, and then, in the second attempt, threw it away. A long shot from back was also tried by Bromley, and this was a capital effort, the ball just grazing the crossbar as it flew over the top. From now to the finish Bromley had much the better of the deal, and few could have been surprised when finally they scored, but their efforts had come too late in the afternoon, and it was not long after their initial success that time came, when the Wanderers had gained the points with a score of 5—1.

Cray Wanderers FC 1860 -2010

Below: Team photo 1907-08. Long-serving full back and "ladies man" the debonair Jack Rogers was now club captain, seated centre of the front row. The evergreen Sack Taylor is back row far left, with goalscorer Jimmy Corke seated directly in front of him. Note the hairstyles in fashion with the youth of St Mary Cray at the time!

However, at the end of the season, it was reported that the Wanderers' accounts were in deficit to the tune of £23 – quite a large sum in those days. The decision was made to continue without the aid of professionalism, for the first time in 13 years. This was a big change for Cray, as they retained amateur status until it was abolished in 1974. It enabled them to re-enter the F.A. Amateur Cup and to play for the first time in the Kent Amateur Cup, which later brought much success and excitement.

1907-08, in fact, turned out to be a very poor season indeed. The Wanderers had slipped well down the local pecking order. In an early friendly game, Bromley, who had suffered miserably for years at Cray's hands, confirmed the new order with a 7-0 victory. Dartford, who beat Cray five times over the campaign, won an exciting match 5-4 in the F.A. Amateur Cup at Fordcroft and the Wanderers made no progress in the Kent Amateur Cup either, losing 3-2 at Rochester, where controversial refereeing decisions cost them the game.

A feature of the season was the number of times that players arrived late for games. For example, the West Kent League game at North Woolwich started with only six Cray players on the pitch! Cray were 0-3 down before the full eleven were present. A suitable comment on a highly forgettable campaign was the fact that the last two games, in late April, were played in thick snow!

At this time, two stalwarts of the side hung up their boots. Jack Rogers was injured in the Cup game with Dartford and did not play again. He had played at full-back throughout the glory days of the turn of the century and was described as being, a terror to an oncoming forward, and a tower of strength … a favourite with the lady supporters. His full-back partner Sack Taylor was playing for the club as early as 1893-94 and was one of the most loyal and long-serving players in the entire history of Cray Wanderers.

Somewhat surprisingly, amidst the doom and gloom, 1908-09 saw something of a revival. The F.A. Amateur Cup holders, Royal Engineers, nar-

rowly beat Cray in the Kent Amateur Cup semi-final. In an even game the Engineers scored a heartbreaking 89th winner, moments after Jimmy Corke hit a post for Cray. Corke was a fine centre-forward, signed from Orpington, who scored 32 goals in the season. He died tragically in 1935 at the age of 50, having sustained an injury at Joynson's Paper Mill, where he worked. Another newcomer to the side was George Shaver Harland, who served the club in many capacities for nearly 70 years.

There was another near-miss for Cray at the end of the season. They finished top of the South Suburban League with the same number of points as Catford Southend, but the Wanderers were defeated 4-1 in a play-off at Orpington's White Hart Ground.

Cray returned to the Kent League in 1909, to play in the Second Division (West), finishing second. They repeated the feat the following year, when they were also runners-up in the West Kent League and champions of the Blackheath League, which was a senior competition.
Cray ventured back into the Kent League's top division in 1911-12 and 1912-13, with little joy. The league was dominated by the reserve sides of Millwall, Gillingham and Crystal Palace. The Wanderers actually beat Palace 3-1 in 1911-12 and got a point in the return fixture, which was something of an achievement. But generally Cray could make little impact against the professional Kent League sides. There was talk in the press of the club turning professional again, or of merging with Orpington, but nothing came of either idea.

The club's cause was not helped by an incident on Boxing Day 1912 when the team, which was two players short, walked off the pitch during a Kent League game at Chatham in the second-half. It is not clear whether this was a deliberate attempt to get the match abandoned, but it led to the suspension of eight of the nine. Cray finished the season bottom of the league. Their final game, at the Den against champions Millwall Reserves, was attended by 4,000.

Although Cray may not always have been a winning team, it seems that they endeavoured to entertain and were rewarded with good support, Eddie Bonwick, himself club secretary in1919, had clear memories in the 1980s of those far-off days before the Great War and players such as Sid Reid, Wally Gillam and Dodger Blackstone as well as Shaver and Wally Heselden. Still turning out for Cray in 1912-13 was Harry Eke, seventeen years after playing for the Wanderers in the Sevenoaks Charity Trophy final at Crystal Palace in 1896.

Eddie recalled one vivid incident when, Sep Reeves took a goal-kick from the Wanderers goal and kicked the ball clean over the visitors' goal posts at the other end without the ball touching the ground.

In 1913-14, Cray returned to the Kent League Second Divison. They also played in the South Suburban League, where they finished fourth to the champions, an up-and-coming team called Charlton Athletic. Charlton beat the Wanderers 5-1 and 4-1, marking the only meetings of the first elevens of the two clubs.

Cray played just one game at the start of the 1914-15 season before operations were suspended due to the war. Too many young men would never return to play or watch another game.

Left: The first sighting of the legendary George 'Shaver' Harland. He is the player far right in the middle row. In the back row the three players are Sep Reeves, Sid Reed (goalkeeper) and the tall Walter Heselden who lost a leg in the First World War.

Chapter 2 - Between The Wars

**Cray Wanderers FC
1860 -2010**

Founded 1860

Into the London League

Some press reports in 1918 suggested that Cray Wanderers F.C. were themselves victims of The Great War that cost so many lives. It was certainly the case that many clubs, including New Crusaders, never re-appeared, but a group of enthusiasts set up a team called Cray Old Boys. The President was local businessman Mr J.T. Fryer and several pre-war Cray Wanderers players were in the side, most notably George Harland, who was the captain, and goalkeeper Sid Reed.

Cray Old Boys entered the 1918-19 Kent Junior Cup and reached the final, only losing to Bexleyheath Labour Club in a replayed final at Bromley. They were also champions of the five-club Sevenoaks & District League, which was not completed until the autumn of 1919.

With football returning to normal, the Old Boys also joined the Darenth Valley and South Suburban Leagues for the 1919-20 season. In effect, Cray Old Boys were the same club as the pre-war Cray Wanderers. Home matches were played at Fordcroft and in June 1920, at a meeting chaired by Fred Brigden, the Wanderers were reconstituted and Cray Old Boys discontinued. Mr Fryer continued as chairman of the club.

Right: Press cutting Sevenoaks & District League 1918 Cray Old Boys.

For the 1920-21 season, the club took the significant step of switching from the mainly professional Kent League to the all-amateur London League. Thus, for the first time ever, Cray's smart new amber and black stripes were seen throughout the whole metropolis, not just Kent and South London. The London League was not considered to be in the very top drawer of amateur football, but even so it was strong enough to produce Leyton, the F.A. Amateur Cup winners in 1926-27, whilst other member clubs such as Barking, Hampstead (Hendon), Mitcham Wanderers, Tooting United (these two clubs merged in 1939) and Wealdstone had fine futures in front of them.

Cray welcomed back some more of their pre-war players, including Sep Reeves, Billy and Charlie Salmon and the veteran Jack Saunders, who again showed irrepressible form on the right wing, although he was hospitalised near the end of the season, suffering from the effects of Hun

FOOTBALL.

DISTRICT LEAGUE MEETING.

A meeting of the District League Committee was held in the Railway and Bicycle Hotel, Sevenoaks, on Tuesday evening, Mr. Bowen (Halstead) in the chair.

Mr. Chase intimated that Eynsford, Brasted and Sundridge, Invicta Motor Works, Tonbridge and Sevenoaks, were all desirous of joining the League. He also intimated that the matches still unplayed were Cray O.B. v. Halstead (home and away matches) and Cray O.B. v. Westerham (home and away matches). Much dissatisfaction was expressed at teams not turning up without a genuine reason. It was latterly decided that Cray O.B. play Halstead a "four points" game on neutral ground, probably at Orpington, on 10th May, and Westerham a similar game at Riverhead on May 7th, thus enabling Cray and Westerham to complete their matches before the close of the season.

On the motion of Mr. Bowen, seconded by Mr. Greenslade, it was decided the following First Division teams be represented at the annual meeting: Halstead, Orpington, Cray, Westerham, Dunton Green, Seal, Sevenoaks, Tonbridge, Hildenborough, Sundridge and Brasted, Eynsford, Eynsford Motor Works, Orpington Local and Holmesdale; and that the following be invited to provide Second Division teams: Otford, Shoreham, Ide Hill, Weald, Sevenoaks Reserve, Knockholt, and Tonbridge Reserve.

It was also agreed that for the season just finishing only the League Shield should be held by the winners and the Cup by the runners-up.

The League Table to date is as follows:—

	P.	W.	L.	D.	F.	A.	Pts.
Halstead	5	5	0	0	20	6	10
Orpington	7	4	2	1	14	9	9
Cray Old Boys	3	2	1	0	8	3	4
Westerham	6	1	4	1	15	19	3
Dunton Green	7	1	6	0	7	22	2

gas. One casualty was Wally Heselden, Cray's left back in 1910-11 and 1911-12 who lost a leg in the war. Seventy years later, at the age of 93, he remained a lively member of the local community and continued to support The Wands. Incidentally, the club's famous and possibly unique nickname was certainly in use at this time and may have been adopted even earlier.

A new club flag was presented by a group of lady supporters and was unfurled on the same flagpole that had been struck by lightning twenty years earlier. A charabanc called The Cray Wanderer was brought into service, although away travel remained rather precarious at times. Mr H.W. Rich, a supporter at Oxford Road in the 1980s, recalled Cray arriving for a game at Catford Southend in the 1920s, in the back of an old furniture van!

On the field, the side made an encouraging start in Division One, the second tier of the London League, finishing 4th. There were some exciting games and a new social trend was reported when Cray met Bromley in a Kent Senior Cup tie on 11th December 1920, watched by nearly 4,000, 'The top corner of the stand was the venue of a chorus of village maidens, who by their enthusiastic urging on of their team, and their chipping of the Bromley men, added much to the gaiety of the occasion. This female enthusiasm for football is evidently a wartime growth, and the girls are clearly not a whit behind the most rabid of men for partisanship'.

S. Chaplin's two goals – including a dramatic last-second equaliser – cancelled out Frank Osborne's two for Bromley. The Boxing Day replay at Bromley brought Cray £291 in gate receipts – a big consolation for an 11-1 defeat before 6,009 spectators, probably the largest crowd ever at a Cray Wanderers game.

Aided in large measure by T.C. Smith's goals (he scored 45 in total), Cray reached the semi-final of the Kent Amateur Cup but lost to Dover after three hard-fought games.

Another excellent campaign in 1921-22 saw Cray finish 3rd and they were elected to the Premier Division. Recruiting players such as Billy Baird (later captain of Bromley, a Kent cap and a Middlesex Wanderer), Bennett (a London League cap) and Alex Butcher made the Wands a strong team, but the top performance of the season was achieved by local lad Billy Salmon who scored all five goals in a 5-2 home win over Wealdstone. There was success for Cray Reserves, too, as they were crowned champions of the Darenth Valley League.

The next three seasons found Cray struggling to hold their own with the top London League clubs. They needed a late rally to avoid relegation in 1923-24. George Harland continued to be the lynchpin of the side, scoring five goals in a Kent Amateur Cup tie against Royal Marines (Deal).

The arrival of several new players brought about a significant improvement from 1925 onwards. Charlie Tomlinson proved to be an intelligent and high-scoring centre-forward, who developed an excellent understanding with Sid Ware at inside-forward. Frank Terry was a fine full-back, who was capped by Kent. At half-back Tommy Banks, joined from Orpington and was a fixture in the side for several seasons. He was one of four brothers who all played for the club.

Ware was top scorer in 1924-25 with 17 goals and the following season Tomlinson scored 30, as Cray improved to 5th place, but the season was marred by outbursts of disorderly conduct by some Cray supporters and an epidemic of foul play on the field. There were squabbles too, amongst the committee, over financial matters. The A.G.M resulted in several resignations.

Cray Wanderers FC
1860 -2010

Founded 1860

***Below**: Team line-up versus Catford Southend in the London League, 1922.*

Match No. 35. GOOD FRIDAY.
Catford Southend Reserves v. Cray Wanderers
LONDON LEAGUE, FIRST DIVISION.

CATFORD TEAM.
(Light and Dark Blue Stripes).

1
H. MOWDAY

RIGHT. LEFT.
2 3
E. LANE. A. T. HILL.
4 5 6
W. J. MARSH. M. P. HUGHES. R. V. HOROBIN.
7 8 9 10 11
R. A. WATKINS. H. S. VALENTINE. W. NICOLLE. H. MILLER. L. F. GOODSELL.

Kick-off 3.30 p.m.

Referee—
Mr. G. W. LEAVER.
London F.A.

12 13 14 15 16
HARLAND. HENDERSON. BUTCHER. SALMON. DEVLIN.
17 18 19
HOAR. BAIRD. KNOWLES.
20 21
NEWMAN. BENNETT.
22
LEFT OTTLEY. RIGHT

CRAY TEAM.
(Amber and Black Stripes.)

**Cray Wanderers FC
1860 -2010**

The Kent Amateur Cup takes centre stage

Cray's intense rivalry with Orpington F.C. – a big factor in local football since the early 1900s – ceased abruptly when The Cockerels fell into decline and folded in 1926. Huge crowds had attended the local derby encounters in previous years, and the usual style of play is evidenced from the report of a 1-1 draw in the Kent Amateur Cup in 1920-21, 'The Cray and Orpington district is noted for its poultry and a good number of 'fouls' were bred on the Wanderers' ground last Saturday.'

Whilst Orpington F.C. would be missed, the crowds still had plenty of excitement, as the Wands began to make a big impact in cup competitions. Although they slipped to 9th place in the league, in 1926-27 Cray reached the F.A. Amateur Cup 1st round proper for the first time. A 4-0 victory over Erith and Belvedere in the final qualifying round earned the Wands a visit to Bromley, but a 3-1 defeat was an anti-climax.

There was also a fine run to the semi-final of the Kent Amateur Cup but Cray were denied at this stage for the third time, losing 1-0 to Royal Naval Depot, in a game played at Dartford.

The 1927-28 season finally saw the Wands achieve their objective of a place in the final of the Kent Amateur Cup. It also brought their closest bid for the London League championship during this period. They led at the halfway stage, but fell away to finish 3rd. One of the results that dented their chances was a 7-2 defeat at Chelmsford in January, when the home side

were awarded four penalties! After the game, Cray's players had to be guarded by the police in their dressing rooms in order to be protected from a mob of Chelmsford supporters. Cray also caused a stir by reaching the Kent Senior Cup semi-final, losing 3-0 to Sittingbourne.

In the Kent Amateur Cup, huge wins over Erith (10-2) and the Loyal Regiment (9-1) led to an epic semi-final versus Bromley. A thrilling 1-1 draw was followed by an equally dramatic replay, played at Erith and Belvedere's ground:

Rain – buckets of it, charas – loads of them, stand – packed, enthusiasm – enormous, mud – pools of water, 3.15 – Kick-off, 3.16 Cray score, BARRELL; 3.45 – Bromley equalise; 3.50 – rain stops; 4.00 half-time. 4.10 – game resumed, 4.11 Cray take lead, TERRY; 4.42 Bromley equalise again from penalty, 4.42½ Cray one up again, WARE; 4.55 – final whistle, pandemonium, and – who's for Dover? All of which means that Cray Wanderers enter the final of the K.A.C. for the first time in their history.

This was the start of a remarkable sequence of four finals in five years for Cray. The occasions were vividly recalled by Ernie Harman:

The final was always played on Easter Monday at Dover. I went by the special train to see the Wands; we had 500 to 600 on each of the trips to Dover and the trams on arrival took us to the famous Crabble Ground where Kent played cricket in the summer.

In fact, Cray played nervously in the 1927-28 final and lost 2-1 to Royal Naval Depot. Then, in the 1928-29 final, Cray were mortified to lose 2-1 to underdogs Whitstable, who fielded six teenagers in their side. Cray, who had beaten the Oystermen 5-1 earlier in the season in the F.A. Cup, were the better team but could not turn their dominance on the day into goals. Both of these finals were watched by crowds in excess of 4,000.

Right: Identifiable in this 1925-26 team photo are manager F Knott (top, far right) and skipper Sid Ware (seated, front row far right).

Cray's form may have been affected by a tragic accident midway through the 1928-29 season when, in a Kent Senior Cup game with Bromley at Fordcroft, club captain Sid Ware was brought down by a heavy tackle and suffered a fractured pelvis. The injury forced him to retire from football. The Orpington Journal commented, 'A harder working, more lion-hearted player never laced a boot.'

A benefit match against London University was arranged for Ware; the programme notes included another tribute, 'Our captain Mr S.E. Ware requires no verbose eulogy, for he can be described adequately by five words – A thorough sportsman and gentleman'.

The injury meant, of course, that Ware's partnership with Tomlinson came to an end. The Cray centre-forward scored 43 goals in 1928-29; he was a player who drew many favourable comments, 'His methods may be quiet, but their effectiveness is shown by the number of times he has found the net...Cool and calculating, he knows where the goal is, and the goalkeeper isn't'.

Cray missed the 1929-30 final and lost in both F.A. competitions away from home to military sides from Chatham, which was a regular occurrence during this period:

Cray are heartily sick of Chatham... the way in which they get drawn against a Chatham service side, and always away from home, is as monotonous as it is remarkable.

The Wands were blessed with some excellent goalkeepers in the 1920s and 1930s: Woodward, Jack Banks, Con Aldridge and Harry Christmas were all players of distinction, the latter an England schoolboy trialist. But against Erith in 1929-30 Cray's 'keeper dropped out at the last moment:

His place in goal was taken by that wonderful veteran 'Shaver' Harland, who performed so well that nothing beat him.

Shaver's dedication to Cray Wanderers continued to know no equals. Ernie Harman remembered how in the 1930s, Cray would sometimes have only ten names in the programme for their

team; the eleventh player would be A.N. Other. The supporters at Fordcroft would speculate whether a new star had been signed. Ten players would come out onto the pitch, the dressing rooms being at the back of the stand. At the last moment, out would come Shaver, rolling up his sleeves and eager to help the team. He was always warmly welcomed by the supporters.

Games in the London League drew attendances of 600-800 to Fordcroft in the 1920s. Away from home, over 4,000 saw Cray win 2-1 at Dagenham in January 1930, whilst a few weeks later, Romford were accompanied to St Mary Cray by, 'A large contingent of supporters who made the air hideous with the continuous and incessant use of rattles.'

The reporter was also perturbed to see that Cray's first scorer was kissed by one of his teammates when celebrating the goal!

It was the 1930-31 season that brought the long-awaited triumph in the Kent Amateur Cup

__Below__: Sid Ware received this letter from the Wands committee, inviting him to continue as club captain in 1927-28.

CRAY WANDERERS FOOTBALL CLUB

Affiliated to the Kent County Football Association
President—CHAS. W. HENDERSON, Esq.

Ground—Fordcroft, St. Mary Cray.   Dressing Rooms on Ground.   Colours—Amber & Black Jerseys, White Knickers.
Nearest Stations—St. Mary Cray (15 minutes) and Orpington (30 minutes) S.R. (S.E. and C. Section).
Headquarters—" BLACK BOY " HOTEL, St. Mary Cray.
Members of the London League—Premier Division and Kent Amateur League (Reserves).

Hon. Sec.—T. HOLMES, 5, Chislehurst Road, Orpington, Kent.
Hon. Treasurer—H. H. ONLEY, 26, Station Road, St. Mary Cray, Kent.
Bankers—Liverpool and Martins, Ltd. (Orpington Branch)

6. August, 192.7.

Dear Mr Ware,

It gives me great pleasure to inform you that the committee have elected you Captain for the ensuing Season in recognition of the magnificent help which you have given to this Club both by your play and your fostering of local talent and spirit in the Team. With your assistance we look forward to a successful and prosperous Season, and we feel sure that you will give us your best endeavours as you have for the past few Seasons.

Yours v. sincerely,

S.E. Ware, Esq.,
Meadow View,
St. Pauls Cray.

Cray Wanderers FC 1860 -2010

Below: A triumphant Cray team after winning the Kent Amateur Cup (actually a shield!) in 1930-31. Players top row L to R: George Miles, Jack Pink, Frank Terry. Middle row: P. May, H. Ellis, Tommy Banks. Front row: Tommy Allchorne, Harry Utz, Harry Reeves, J. Banks, H. Clachan. The officials include W. Skinner (trainer, with towel over his shoulder) and F. Knott (manager, next to Tommy Banks).

(which was actually a shield!). En route to the final, the Wands defeated both the Naval Depot and the Marines from Chatham, before beating the holders Aylesford Paper Mills 3-0 before 3,073 spectators at Dover. Harry Utz, Alf Banks and Harry Reeves netted the goals. During the celebrations, one could reflect on the romance of Alf Banks, aged 39, playing his first ever season of senior football, whilst his nephew Tommy Allchorne, aged 18, was sprinting up and down Cray's right wing.

Like all good sides, Cray's success was based on a very strong spine. Ahead of Con Aldridge in goal, the full-backs were the long-serving George Miles and Frank Terry, who had taken over from two very accomplished players: former captain Lohse, who signed for Northampton and George Dumbrell, who later played League football for Brentford and Leicester City. Tommy Banks was the best of the half-backs, with sharpshooting Harry Reeves at centre-forward.

Reeves, who was capped 30 times for Kent, recalls the soccer tactics of his day:

All five forwards stayed up the field, and the defenders stayed back. I can't remember ever tackling an opposing player. I was probably the 'greediest' player there ever was! But that was the style of play, to try and dribble round all the opposing men – the idea was to get the ball and keep it for as long as you could!

Reeves also paid tribute to the Cray treasurer, Mr Harry Sands, who gave tremendous financial support to the club.

Cray Reserves also had a successful campaign. They reached the divisional final of the Kent Junior Cup, losing 1-0 to Clarence Guild (Gravesend) at Millwall's Den in front of a remarkable crowd of 3,500. Jack Pink played brilliantly in goal for the Wands. The Reserves did win the Kent Amateur League Division Two Benevolent (League) Cup, a feat they repeated the following season.

Cray returned to Dover again in the Kent Amateur Cup final in 1932, but injuries forced them to field a much weakened side in the final, and they were swept aside 4-1 by Bromley.

Depression takes a hold

Apart from the Kent Amateur Cup run, the 1931-32 season was a poor one. Early exits from both F.A. competitions (including another defeat at Chatham's Naval Depot in the Amateur Cup!) affected income, while a spate of injuries, as well as the loss of some key players, led to a decline in form in the London League. Harry Utz, who played in France for the League's representative team against the Paris League at the Stade Buffalo, turned out for the Wands at inside-forward, goalkeeper and centre-half in successive games! Cray finished next-to-bottom in 1931-32 and the following season was mediocre, with the most notable event occurring in an F.A. Amateur Cup tie with Catford Wanderers at Fordcroft. The Wands were awarded a penalty in extra time with the score 1-1, but the Cray players thought the offence had taken place outside the area. Sportingly, George Miles made no attempt to score from the spot, rolling the ball gently to the goalkeeper. Catford won the replay 3-1.

Then, in 1933-34 Cray found themselves rooted to the bottom of the table. A record defeat at runaway league leaders Park Royal (14-1) was bad enough, but most embarrassing of all was a charity game played on Easter Saturday

CRAY WANDERERS TEAM 1930.

in aid of the St Mary Cray Unemployment Fund. In a serious challenge match between the Wands first team and the Reserves, the senior side were thrashed 7-2, with Jumbo Collins, a skilful and powerful inside-forward, scoring a hat-trick.

In complete contrast to the first team, the Reserves had another excellent season, finishing 4th in the Kent Amateur League and winning the Benevolent Shield (League Cup), beating champions Swanley Athletic 4-2 after extra-time in the final at Welling. It appears, though, that Cray Reserves were completely isolated from the first team, with a completely different set of players and officials. They were disbanded at the end of the season, with the very strange explanation: 'The Reserves have had no connection with Cray Wanderers for the past few years and have been using a name to which they were not entitled.'

The local press decided it was time to start some stirring. A hard-hitting article drew attention to proposed changes in the structure of senior amateur football in the south, which would benefit progressive clubs, but might endanger the future of clubs like Cray, who appeared to be stuck in a rut. When the club committee replied that financial shortage was the cause of the Wands' stagnation, the local press expressed sympathy for the small group of loyal workers and fund raisers, but chastised them for passing over good local players and wasting money on 'outsiders' who promised much but delivered little. They pointed out too that the Wands had failed to attract support from the fast-growing population of Orpington. No doubt the financial Depression was a factor, but attendances had dropped to around 250.

It was probably fair comment that the Wands had been gently dozing off to sleep for a few years. But the club reawoke with a bold explosion after the 1933-34 A.G.M., when it was announced that they would withdraw from the London League, and would re-enter the Kent League for 1934-35.

This was a high-risk strategy for a club struggling to hold its own in amateur circles. In those days, the Kent League was a strong, mainly professional competition, and the precedents were not good for amateur clubs trying to take part. But Cray spurned the cautious choice of entering

Division Two, comprised of other amateur clubs such as Chatham and Whitstable. On the theory that better opposition would attract bigger gates and improve the finances of the club, the Wands plunged bravely into Division One.

Some rousing speeches were made at the A.G.M., and additional finance was pledged by committee members and supporters. Even so, photographs from the period betray the fact that Cray were one of the Kent League's poor relations. The players' kit looked distinctly tatty; so too the Fordcroft ground where the London League had in fact demanded improvement of the dressing rooms. Tommy Allchorne recalled: Some of the Kent League clubs had wonderful facilities, especially Margate and Northfleet (respectively the nursery clubs of Arsenal and Spurs). At Cray we had just one single bath; the players had to take turns one by one after the game. It wasn't so bad if you were one of the first ones in, but gradually the bath would fill up with mud!

Cray made an encouraging start to their return to the Kent League. There was a new wave of enthusiasm, as the committee secured the services of several new players. The most important of these was Bill Inglis, who had played for Reading and four other Football League clubs. A giant of a man, he played at centre-half and was skipper. His professional know-how was a great asset on the field, and he helped develop the young wing halves Dicky Price and Bobby Lintott (who stepped up from the Reserves). Allchorne, Miles and Reeves remained in the team; on the left wing, young Walter Imms had speed and skill, and Harry Wood had a productive season at centre-forward, scoring 40 goals.

Amongst Cray's best results in 1934-35 were successive home victories in January, over Margate in the league and Ashford in the Kent Senior Cup. Cray's goalkeeper, George Barron, was described as first class in the latter game. Barron was one of the Wands' best-ever 'keepers and played a big role in the club's successful first two seasons back in the Kent League. He then moved to Northfleet, the Spurs' nursery side and did, in fact, play one first team game for Tottenham, a war-time Football League match at Reading. But George's opportunities for progress were restricted by the arrival at Northfleet of Ted Ditchburn, who became an England international

Cray Wanderers FC
1860 -2010

Founded 1860

after the war. George remained amateur and played for Erith & Belvedere and Bromley. He was said to be 'the man widely regarded as the finest amateur goalkeeper in England'. George's son, Paul Barron, was Crystal Palace's 'keeper for several seasons.

A run of defeats, caused by fixture congestion at the end of the season, saw Cray drop to 17th out of the 19 in the league, but 7th place in 1935-36 was arguably the Wands' best league performance between the wars, considering the standard of opposition encountered in the Kent League. The early results were awful, including a 12-0 defeat at Canterbury. But the team later improved their form, and the local press summarised the season favourably, 'On the whole, the football seen at Fordcroft has been good. Cray is one of the oldest clubs in Kent, yet it is poorly patronised. The committee have got together a good team'.

It is true that attendances, at around 350, had not improved as much as had been hoped, but, at the end of 1935-36, one could reasonably conclude that Cray's gamble in joining the Kent League had paid off. Mr Joynson arranged for water to be laid on at the ground, prompting the *Kentish Times* to comment that he 'Deserves a full tribute in any history of the club that may be written'.

The wind seemed to be set fair for the good ship Cray Wanderers to sail forth successfully. In fact, a torpedo was on its way to blow the club out of the water, condemning the Wands

to fifteen years of misery and near-extinction. Ironically, it was Mr Joynson's decision to put Fordcroft, Cray's home ground since 1898, up for sale, that led to the crisis. Mr Joynson had retired in 1930 and sold his business to Wiggins Teape & Co and a Belgian company, who converted the mill to produce greaseproof paper and vegetable parchment. This involved the temporary closure of the mill and the loss of scores of jobs. Mr Joynson's decision to sell Fordcroft and leave the area was announced in June 1936.

Why didn't Cray ever attempt to buy the ground? Ernie Harman recalled that 'Cray had paid such a small rent annually that no one ever thought about buying it. All the time Mr. Joynson lived behind the ground he would not sell anyway.' Cray kicked off the 1936-37 season still at Fordcroft. Most of the better players left, Barron to Northfleet, as a trialist for Spurs, and Allchorne, Imms, Price, Lintott and Wood all went to Maidstone. This gave promising young players such as full-back Bob Ganfield their opportunity, but they found the going extremely hard and the Wands had not won a league game by the end of October. To make matters worse, thieves raided Fordcroft and stole the club's three footballs!

Cray's final match at Fordcroft was played on November 7th 1936. The sadness of leaving a ground that had been home to the club for nearly forty years was relieved, to some extent, by the first Kent League victory of the season, 3-2 against Ashford. The Wands then moved reluctantly to Twysdens Meadow, Footscray, close to the site of the later Schweppes/Coca-Cola

Right: The Cray team that started a short-lived new era in the Kent League in 1934-35. They lost 2-1 to Sheppey United in the first game. Back row (L to R): Dicky Price, Tommy Allchorne, Bobby Lintott, George Barron, Harry Ellis, Arthur Service. Front row: Darkie Turrell, Paul Schofield, Harry Wood, J Mandy, Harry Reeves.

drinks factory. A curious feature of the ground was a hump running the length of the field caused by an underground water pipe! Margate were the first visitors and they won 6-0 and had Jack Lambert, the old Arsenal and England centre forward, in their team.

One of the few light-hearted moments of this season occurred during the 8-1 home defeat by Bexleyheath on Boxing Day, involving Cray's goalkeeper, G. H. Jowers. The local press related that in a game reduced to farce by fog, When Jowers took a goal-kick, referee Chapman evidently could not see the ball, which struck his head and laid him out. He recovered after attention from the trainers.

There was not much else to laugh at. The Wands were cast hopelessly adrift at the bottom of the Kent League, conceding 164 goals.

Left: George Barron in action for Cray versus London Paper Mills in a Kent League game at Fordcroft.

The following season was equally as abysmal; Cray were bottom again and only picked up one point away from home in 16 games. For 1938-39, the committee took the sensible decision to drop a level, abandoning the Kent League for the Kent Amateur League. Cray fans, who were by now thin on the ground, must have wondered if the nightmare would ever end, after a shock 10-0 home defeat against Northfleet Amateurs in the first match. However, this dreadful result appears to have been something of a freak. After a few changes Cray emerged as one of the stronger sides in the league.

Left: Cray v Bexley 13.9.35 action photo at Fordcroft Might this be Bill Inglis? – looks like a colossus of a defender heading the ball!

Cray Wanderers FC 1860 -2010

Founded 1860

During this season, George Miles' impressive career with Cray came to a close after 13 years. Harry Reeves, a great admirer of Miles, recalled: 'George Miles was a splendid player; he was so strong, he made tremendous tackles. He was never beaten; if someone got round him, he would recover and get back.'

Early inconsistency put Cray out of serious contention for the league, but the team's form improved considerably in the New Year. The Wands' cup performances were vastly better than the two previous seasons, and they reached the final of the League Cup, losing 2-0 to champions, Darenth Park after extra-time at Bexleyheath. This was a competition won by Cray's Reserves just five years earlier - an indication of how rapidly the club's status had fallen.

Right: Cray versus Callendars at Twysdens 1937-38.

There was much doubt and anxious discussion during the close season. The club's officials announced that support at Twysdens had been so poor that they did not see how the club could continue, unless a return to St Mary Cray could be arranged. They offered to hand over the club to any parties who could find a suitable new ground. This was not forthcoming but, perhaps in a rather desperate attempt to attract more local support, the club's name was changed to Sidcup and Footscray F.C. for the 1939-40 season, which began at Twysdens.

The declaration of war meant an immediate curtailment of competition, although within a few weeks the 'Sidcup Wartime Football Competition' started. Cray were fortunate enough to have nearly all the previous season's team available, winning 7 of 10 fixtures in the competition and losing only once, to eventual champions, Trojans F.C. There were some very high scoring games, including a 17-2 victory against Lamorbey Social, one W. Rose scoring 8 goals!

Right: Fog – Cray versus Bexleyheath & Welling at Twysdens 1936-37.

Cray also entered the London Senior Cup, losing 3-0 to Barking in a game that, significantly, was played at Grassmeade, in St Mary Cray,.

In the dark days of 1940 local football more or less went into hibernation. With no ground, very little support and even the historic name no longer in use, the future looked extremely bleak for Cray Wanderers.

Chapter 3 – Back to St Mary Cray

The dark days of the 1940s

In the autumn of 1941, a war-time Cray Football League was established. One of the members, Vegpardel, the works team of the St Mary Cray Vegetable Parchment Mills, was far superior to the others. The driving force behind the Vegpardel club was George Shaver Harland.

In 1942-43 Vegpardel played in the South London Alliance, which included the likes of Woolwich Poly, Erith & Belvedere and VCD Athletic. Harry Reeves, by now a veteran, occasionally turned out for the team and was a source of inspiration to the younger players. Most of the Vegpardel's home games were played at Grassmeade and the club fought their way to the final of the Kent Junior Cup, where they lost narrowly to one of the many Service teams in the competition.

Then, in September 1943, it was announced in the Sidcup and District Times that 'Vegpardel have changed their name to Cray Wanderers.'

Quite how a works side could take over the name of one of the county's most famous senior clubs is not entirely clear, but many things are possible when a war is on that would be against the rules in peacetime! It seems likely that Cray Wanderers had all but ceased to exist in 1940. George Harland saw an opportunity to re-establish the club back in their historic home area and he used his Vegpardel works team as the basis for reviving the club he had served for over thirty years. There was a strong connection with the past, as the Vegetable Parchment Mill had previously been the mill owned by Mr Joynson, the club's benefactor until 1936.

A great debt of gratitude is therefore owed to Shaver for ensuring that Cray Wanderers survived the war, unlike a number of senior clubs. Bert Booker offered this tribute to him, 'The greatest man of all in Cray Wanderers history is George Shaver Harland. His heart and soul were in the club. He was also a fine cornet player; he played in the town band, and he taught the youngsters how to play. After he retired from playing football, he did everything for Cray – he was manager, trainer, groundsman.'

So the name of Cray Wanderers appeared in football results for the 1943-44 season, for the first time in four years. The team was very much the same as the one that had played under the name of Vegpardel during the previous campaign.

During this season, possibly the most famous player ever to represent the Wands made his mark - Jimmy Sanders, a young goal-keeper who had previously played for Longlands Athletic. He had been signed by Charlton in 1940 as an understudy to the great Sam Bartram; both men served in the R.A.F. during the war. Jimmy was an air gunner in the Middle East, but was shot down, sustaining neck and back injuries. He was told he would never play football again.

Returning to the area to recuperate, Jimmy played a few games for Cray starting in November 1943. His performance for the Wands in a Kent Senior Cup tie against Millwall Reserves at The Den in January 1944 was sensational. Ernie Harman, who was there, said 'We should have lost 8-1, but Sanders played a blinder! We got a breakaway goal and Sanders made save after save.'

Reg Morfill, who scored Cray's goal, recalled that 'After the game our dressing room was invaded by Millwall officials anxious to sign our goalkeeper. At that time, however, Jim was on Charlton's books, and used to turn out for Charlton when Sam Bartram was not available.'

Cray Wanderers FC 1860 -2010

Below: Heroics in goal from Jim Sanders at The Den in 1944.

**Cray Wanderers FC
1860 -2010**

Sanders was transferred from Charlton to West Bromwich Albion at the end of the war. He made 391 appearances for The Baggies, including the 1954 F.A. Cup final, when West Brom beat Preston 3-2.

Ironically, because Cray could not find a ground for the replay with Millwall, they had to forfeit the tie. They did, however, reach the final of the Kent Junior Cup again, but lost 3-0 to the Searchlight Battery at Grassmeade.

The Wands competed in the South London Alliance for the next two seasons, finishing as runners-up in 1945-46. In 1946-47 the Kent Amateur League re-started. George Harland was the club secretary, but many of the best local players were to be found playing for Cray's near rivals, such as Bob Ganfield, who now captained the very successful Footscray Social club. Cray finished second from bottom. Playing for the Wanderers around this time were Haydn Diggins and Arthur Styles, whose sons Barry and Howard played for Cray in the mid-1960s. Haydn later became first team trainer and Arthur reserve team manager.

The 1947-48 season was approached with optimism but this quickly evaporated as the club was hit by an exodus of officials and players. The source of this crisis was once more ground insecurity. It is probably best that a veil is drawn over the circumstances surrounding the loss of Grassmeade, but the bare facts are that the owners of the site, St Philomena's School, decided that the area should be devoted exclusively to educational purposes and asked the Wanderers and the Gas Sports Guild (with whom they shared) to vacate the site. Having effectively evicted the Wands, the school authorities appear to have made a U-turn and leased the ground to another club.

Cray again finished second from bottom in 1947-48. In 1948-49 they found themselves on St Mary Cray Recreation Ground. The performance of the team became almost a secondary issue to the search for a new ground. Voluminous correspondence has survived, which confirms that the committee did everything that one could reasonably ask in this endeavour, but with no success.

The team's results on the field were heartbreaking at this stage. Callenders Athletic inflicted the two worst defeats in the club's history (15-2 and 14-0) as the Wands finished bottom of the Kent Amateur League with just seven points. George Harland's report as secretary to the AGM is recorded in just 19 terse words, 'Mr Harland stated that the past season had been the worst season he had ever known. Financially and playing.'

In August 1949 Shaver, who had already relinquished the Secretaryship, did the unthinkable and resigned from the committee. For a man of his loyalty to make such a decision underlines the gravity of the situation.

OUR LOCAL FOOTBALLERS: K.T. SERIES

The "Kentish Times" will be glad to include photographs of North-West Kent football teams in this new series. Senior and junior clubs will be included, and there will be no priority in the order in which pictures are published.

Club secretaries who would like their teams to be included in the series are invited to notify the Editor. (1) Where the photograph may be taken, (2) the time, (3) two or three suitable dates. The Editor will confirm the arrangements.

NO. 4.—CRAY WANDERERS

Back row, left to right, G. Harland (secretary), F. Jones (trainer), R. Wright, A. W. Sleafer, A. V. Jones, C. Hills, F. Curtis, G. Bennett (manager); front row, left to right, J. Phillips, F. Dunn, K. O. Jones (captain), G. Mansfield, J. Keating.

Right: Team photo 1947-48

The 1949-50 season saw Cray come to within a hairs-breadth of extinction, with only four or five active committee members. At the beginning of November 1949 three committee meetings were abandoned because they were inquorate and the three members present agreed to settle all outstanding debts in anticipation of the worst. Cray Wanderers had, to all intents and purposes, ceased to exist at the third of these meetings! Thankfully, with the support of the players the club continued, and it is to Secretary A.J. Hanson and his handful of colleagues that we today owe a vote of thanks.

Mick Slater takes over

The summer of 1950 saw a series of events that completely transformed the outlook for Cray Wanderers. Some new blood was co-opted into the management of the club, including a Mr Dowding as treasurer, and George Harland agreed to resume on the committee. Furthermore, the Gas Sports Guild had negotiated a lease on a pitch at Northfield Farm. The site is now housing – Northfield Avenue and Sussex Avenue. Although far from perfect (on more than occasion the farm manager left the entrance locked on the day of a match!), it would certainly be an improvement to playing on the St Mary Cray Rec.

Then, in August, events took a sudden and unexpected twist. Mr Dowding announced that a five-strong group led by Michael Slater had offered to invest £50 each into the club if total control were given to them. After two public meetings, the offer was accepted unanimously and a new era dawned for the club. Mick Slater had already shown his ability as a sporting entrepreneur, with a genuine concern for the youth of Orpington and the Crays. He had established the Cray Tigers cycle speedway club, who raced at a cinder track he had made at Hackett Jones' Farm, and they were almost unbeatable.

Of Mick's other colleagues, Mr Mills became Chairman, Mr Pearce was made Press Officer and Tom Forrester was team manager. MP Sir Waldron Smithers was the new patron of the club; he attended the first game at Northfield, which was lost 3-1 to Footscray Social. Although early results were poor, the team's fortunes improved dramatically once some experienced signings were made. Cray also somewhat ruthlessly acquired many of the best players from their local rivals.

CLUB NOTES

———

WELCOME to NORTHFIELD the new home of The Old Wanderers. We hope to take the old club up and regain its former glory, to attain this, Ladies and Gentlemen, we need your support. As the oldest club in Kent, we feel sure you with us, will be proud if we can reach that object. We have'nt any magic at our disposal, and we ask you to be patient for a short time to enable us to build a team, those of you who know something of the club will appreciate the difficulties we have to surmount, but with your support we will do our utmost to BRING FOOTBALL BACK TO CRAY.

Cheerio Folks,

see you all next week,

The Wanderer.

CRAY WANDERERS v FOOTS CRAY SOCIAL

SATURDAY, SEPTEMBER 16th 1950

Any changes in the teams will be announced over the loud-speaker

———————————————————

CRAY WANDERERS
Colours: Amber & Black

RIGHT   LEFT

G. PRICE

C. BOOKER   J. NEWLAND

B. KERSWELL   A. SLEAPER   P. KEVIN

D. WHATLEY   J. WALLER   J. DOUGALS   J. IMMS   J. WAY

O

J. COVILL   A. HOARE   A. BALL   M. McNALLY   H. HILLS

J. WATSON   J. BUGDEN   P. REYNOLDS

J. STEVENS   S. BACKHOUSE

K. R. SKEGG

LEFT   RIGHT

FOOTS CRAY SOCIAL
Colours: Claret & Yellow

———————————————————

Left: New management and a new ground (although only for one year) as the Wands are "reborn" in 1950-51 under Mick Slater.

Cray Wanderers FC
1860 -2010

From mid-January 1950, 12 games in a row were won, including a 7-1 victory over Footscray – the first win over these local rivals in 19 attempts! Cray finished 1950-51 as runners up in the Kent Amateur League, reached the semi-final of the League Cup and had two players, George Price and Tommy Lee, chosen for Kent – an extraordinary contrast to the events of the previous season.

The lease at Northfields was only for a year's duration, but almost immediately a three-year lease on the Rowlands Manor site (nowadays the site of the Roman Catholic Church) was secured. It was typical of Mick Slater's flair for publicity to call the new ground Fordcroft, as it was adjacent to the original Fordcroft. Mr A. J. Tatham, the club president, paid the £500 needed to prepare the site for football.

Mick obtained Cray's election back into the London League for the 1951-52 season, after a break of 17 years. The first two campaigns were one of consolidation. The highlights of 1951-52 were two victories away to Dartford Reserves, in front of crowds of over 1,000.

Below: A 3-1 win for Cray at Beckenham in January 1955 recorded in a Syd Jordan cartoon.

The new Fordcroft ground, which was also known as Tothills, caused some problems for the Wands. Due to its proximity to the River Cray, it was prone to waterlogging at one end. Worse still, a game at home to Dartford in November 1951 had to be abandoned at half-time when, rain caused glass and flint to appear on the pitch.

Cray became a really strong team again in 1953-54 when they recruited Bromley's veteran wingers Cyril Martin and Martin Ruddy. Martin, an England amateur international, stayed briefly as player manager, but Ruddy remained a very popular first team regular until 1956-57, when he was reportedly aged in his mid-forties.

During the season, Mick Slater rented the Grassmeade ground for midweek matches, which were made possible by the floodlights he had installed there. This started a remarkable episode in the Wands' history, as Mick claimed that the Wands were the first amateur club in the whole of England to be staging floodlit football matches. Huge crowds came to see the evening games in 1953-54 and 1954-55. Floodlit football was an exciting novelty for the public and Cray arranged some prestige fixtures against the likes of Dartford and Sutton. Fog unfortunately caused a few cancellations, and then one night a fierce storm destroyed the lights for good.

Cray were London League runners-up in 1953-54. The biggest game of the season was a 2nd round Kent Amateur Cup tie against Bromley. A huge crowd, reported to be between 3,000 and 4,000 descended on Fordcroft. This is probably the largest home attendance in the Wands' history. The fairground site in Cray Avenue (now a boating pool) was converted into a temporary car park. Bromley were made to fight every inch of the way, before winning 1-0.

Staying at Fordcroft for a fourth season, Cray exchanged their black jerseys with amber sleeves for plain amber shirts in 1954-55. They had their best ever start to a season when they won nine successive games, but three defeats in four matches early in the New Year cost them the title, as they finished just one point behind Aveley. Bromley visited Fordcroft again, this time in the semi-final of the Kent Amateur Cup, winning comfortably 4-0.

The season ended in triumph when Beckenham were beaten 3-1 in the London League Cup final at Hayes Lane. It was an occasion of pride for Mick Slater to savour – Cray's first major trophy since 1930-31 and a sign of better things to come.

The team was led by Joe Harris, a fine centre-half who later starred for Maidstone and was a Kent cap. Bill Bedwell, who scored over 100 goals for the club, and Les Butterfill, both forwards, were to be two of Cray's most loyal servants throughout the 1950s. Alan Viney, a skilful ball-playing inside forward, went on to fame with Bromley and Tooting, whilst Jim Emblen was a resolute defender and an excellent penalty-taker; he converted 17 spot-kicks in two seasons. This was also the start of Ken Collishaw's legendary goal-scoring era. From his debut in 1954 to his retirement caused by injury in 1965, he netted 274 first team goals – the club record total. His 57-goal tally in 1956-57 is the record for an individual season.

Collishaw was a truly outstanding player. He was extremely robust and he packed a really power-ful shot which he liked to use whenever the goal came in sight. He had the priceless gift of timing the ball as he went in for headers near goal. His approach play was also very clever; he had tremendous ball control and could weight a pass beautifully.

When other centre forwards might have been content with a hat-trick, Ken often went on to score four, five or six goals in a game, He twice scored seven: the occasions were a 10-1 win against Basildon in the London League in 1957-58 and 9-1 victory over Sheppey in the Kent Amateur Cup in 1959-60. Another club record he holds is scoring in eight consecutive games in 1957-58.

Below: *After winning the London League Cup at Bromley F.C. in 1954-55, defeating Beckenham 3-1 in the final. Back row (L to R): Nat Kennell, Alan Viney, Peter Verge, Freddie Noakes, Les Butterfill, Ken Collishaw. Front row: Martin Ruddy, Colin Crowther, Joe Harris, Jim Emblen, Bill Bedwell.*

**Cray Wanderers FC
1860 -2010**

*Below: Back row (L to R): Jim Emblen, Colin Crowther, John Rosser, Brian Dunmall, Ron Knock, Mick Slater.
Front row: D Pearson, T Nicholls, Les Butterfill, Bill Bedwell, Freddie Noakes, Martin Ruddy.*

Return to Grassmeade

Cray finally moved in full-time at Grassmeade for the 1955-56 season. They again did well, finishing third in the London League, Bedwell top scoring with 27 goals. A sign of Mick Slater's growing ambition for the club was the withdrawal of the Cray's entry into the Kent Amateur Cup for this and the following season in protest at the Kent F.A. expecting the Wands to play through the qualifying rounds.

The real breakthrough came in 1956-57, when Cray swept to the London League championship. Collishaw was on fire; he had one sequence of 15 goals in 5 games! An unbeaten run of 16 games (14 wins and 2 draws) in the second half of the season secured the title. The run ended disappointingly when the Wands lost to Wingate in a bruising replay of the London League Cup final, but a few days later, Cray celebrated winning the Bromley Hospital Cup, beating Bromley 3-2 at Hayes Lane.
The season featured some remarkable high scoring games. Wins against Chingford by 11-1, Wingate 10-1, Harlow 9-3 and Epping 8-0 and defeats to Cheshunt by 8-5, Wokingham 8-3 and Maidstone 7-2 are only a few examples! Cray's rather leaky defence became considerably tighter when young Johnny Day was tried out at centre-half in January. Day made an immediate impact, and soon had Football League scouts flocking to Grassmeade to see him.

In 1957-58 Cray comfortably retained the London League title. They did not lose a league game until the end of March, an unbeaten run of 31 matches since December 1956. A deserved 2-0 victory over Bromley in the Kent Senior Cup, Sid Talbot scoring both the goals, was possibly the best result of the whole 1950s decade. The Wands won the Bromley Hospital Cup again, this time on the toss of a coin, after a draw at Hayes Lane.

Johnny Day moved on to Bromley a few weeks into the season, on the advice of England amateur international selectors, who thought he might be a potential cap.

The local football community was stunned when Johnny collapsed and died during a park game in May 1958 – a tragic and untimely death at the age of 24. Cray supporter Donald (Ted) Ward, a writer with several books of poetry published, dedicated his poem 'The Footballer' to Johnny Day. It includes these words:

Each invading thrust
Tethered to his eye,
He moves across the line
Focused and supreme.

Deep in the field he broods,
He stands so beautifully,
Foot and body poised
To the instant need.

An altogether different type of defender was the rugged Bert Howe, who played a few games for Cray at the end of the 1957-58 season. He went on to make nearly 200 Football League appearances for Crystal Palace.

Cray were troubled by injuries in 1958-59 and did well to finish 3rd in the league, mainly due to a good run in mid-season when a new inside forward trio of Fred Shaw, Tommy Kerner and John Buffoni had a brief flourish. The season included Cray's first ever competitive game under floodlights, a 2-1 defeat at Maidstone in a Kent Senior Cup replay.

Cray left the London League in 1959-60 and went into the newly-founded Aetolian League, which included several clubs from the disbanded Kent League. This was a compromise for Mick Slater, who really wanted to get Cray into one of the fashionable amateur leagues such as the Athenian or Corinthian. Alas, Cray's applications to join these leagues were repeatedly rejected. Mick hoped that the Aetolian would offer more scope for advancement than the London League. In fact, it soon transpired that the two leagues were much of a muchness, and when they both suffered diminishing numbers in the early 1960s, they were forced to merge in 1964-65 under the name of the Greater London League.

**Cray Wanderers FC
1860 -2010**

Below: London League Champions 1956-7 with the Dewar Shield. Back row (L to R): Reg Davies, Harry Wager, Harry Pocock, Les Rawle, Johnny Day. Front row: Sid Talbot, Les Butterfill, Ken Collishaw, Bob Allen, Alan Basham, Martin

**Cray Wanderers FC
1860 -2010**

*Right: Syd Jordan's
cartoon records that Cray
were too strong for the
Charlton Athletic 'A' side
in 1960-61.*

*Below: Cray and
Crockenhill players line
up for a minute's silence
at Wested Meadow on
the death of Crockenhill's
President Mr Miller.
Photo: Courtesy of
Crockenhill FC*

Nevertheless, the five years in the Aetolian were a backcloth for some successful exploits by the Wands. 1959-60 was a poor season, although Cray did reach the Kent Amateur Cup final for the first time in nearly 30 years. Unfortunately, Cray suffered a catalogue of injuries prior to the game and had to field a terribly depleted side, some of whom were far from fit. Bromley trounced them 7-3.

1960-61 saw two changes at the start of the season: a new kit of amber shirts and amber shorts and a return to the F.A. Cup for the first time since the war. A crowd of over 1,000 at Grassmeade saw Dartford win a thrilling game 5-4. Cray were

third in the league and had an exciting run to the semi-final of the Kent Senior Cup, where they lost 5-1 in a local derby at Bexleyheath and Welling before a crowd of 2,621.

In the league game at Deal, Cray took the field with just 8 men, after a car carrying three players broke down. They arrived by taxi after the game had been in progress for 15 minutes; the score was still 0-0 and the Wands went on to win 3-1. The season also included the most remarkable own goal ever seen in a Cray game. The Eton Manor keeper cleared the ball to his left winger; he passed to the left half, who played the ball back to the left back Ballard. In attempting a back pass, Ballard lobbed the 'keeper and scored. No Cray player touched the ball in the entire move!

Cray finished the season 3rd in the league and also reached the final of the Southern Combination Cup, losing 5-4 to Windsor and Eton. At the AGM, a proposal to change the club's name to Orpington and Cray F.C. was defeated. Mick Slater, in particular, was adamant that the historic name of Cray Wanderers should be preserved.

Cray's dull 1961-62 season was notable only for the arrival of a new centre-half, John Dorey. A fine player and a true sportsman, Dorey went on to skipper the Wands through one of the most successful ten-year phases of their history. A

Kent cap, he made approximately 500 first team appearances, which is probably the club record total. Other players coming into the reckoning are Harry Hutchins, Jack Rogers and Sack Taylor from the early days, George Miles from between the wars and, most recently, Ian Jenkins, but it is not possible to compare their totals with complete accuracy.

Cup Fever

In terms of the numbers of trophies won and the prominence the club gained in national cup competitions, the period from 1962 to 1969 was the most successful in the history of Cray Wanderers.

In 1962-63, the Wands reached the 1st round proper of the F.A. Amateur Cup for the first time since 1926-27; coincidentally, as was the case 36 years earlier, a home victory over Erith & Belvedere secured their passage. There was a prolonged winter freeze before Cray could play their 1st round game at Barnet; in common with most teams, the Wands played no football for two months. In a desperate attempt to thaw the ice and snow, Barnet bought tons of old car tyres, set them alight and dragged them around the pitch! It was all to no avail. The game had to be played at Enfield's ground, and Cray lost 3-0.

Cray Wanderers FC
1860 -2010

Founded 1860

Below: The Wands in an all-red kit during season 1961-62. Players in the back row (L to R) John Miles, George Cornish, John Dorey, Ron Vosper in goal, Peter Clark, Dan Merron. In the front row first left Dick Roythorne with team manager Arthur Barron beside him, next players Eric Jones, Micky Harrington, Ted Clarke, John Jackson.

Cray Wanderers FC 1860 -2010

Founded 1860

Right: *Ken Collishaw retired in 1965 with 274 goals to his name. Ken (right) is pictured here with Micky Harrington.*

Below: *Kent Amateur Cup winners 1962-63. Back row (L to R): Arthur Barron, Ted Clarke, Alan Sterling, Stan Matthews, Ted Vibert, Mick Slater. Front: Alan Viney, Ray Hutchins, Nick Howe, John Dorey, Micky Thompson, Johnny Stevens.*

In the Kent Amateur Cup, Cray saw off three of the strongest amateur clubs in the county – Herne Bay, Erith and Faversham – to reach the Good Friday final against Bromley at Hayes Lane. It seemed like a huge setback for the Wands when Ken Collishaw suffered a training injury on the morning of the match, but his replacement Neville Rappold, making his debut for the club, played like a hero in Cray's magnificent 3-1 win, attendance 3,567.

Faced with a huge fixture pile-up, Cray embarked on a tremendous unbeaten run (16 games) in the Aetolian League, snatching the championship on the very last day of the season, at the end of May, with a 3-1 win at Herne Bay, their main rivals. Alan Viney, described as that wonderful touch player in the Kent Messenger, scored two of the goals. The Wands were then invited on a short tour of Luxembourg and West Germany, where they won both games.

In 1963-64, Cray confirmed their position as one of the most feared clubs in Kent, as they settled scores with Dartford in the F.A. Cup (1-0) and again beat Bromley in Kent Amateur Cup at Hayes Lane (also 1-0, in the quarter-final).

Their league form stuttered a little after Collishaw sustained a long-term injury in a cup-tie with Woolwich Poly, but the Wands continued to flourish in the cups.

**Cray Wanderers FC
1860 -2010**

Left:: Brian Hill scores for Cray versus Epping Town in 1965.

Below: Team photo 1965-66 with the Orpington Hospital Cup, Greater London League Cup and Kent Amateur Cup. Back row (L to R): Alan Taylor, Billy Smith, George Wittey, Peter Warner, Alan Howe, Peter Clark. Front row: Len Kenny, Carlo Nastri, John Dorey, Brian Hill, Gerry Whooley.

The Kent Amateur Cup was retained, beating Herne Bay 4-2 in the final, and they added the Aetolian League Cup, beating Chatham 4-3 in an exciting final at Sheppey. Cray also beat Chatham 4-1 to win the early season Rowland Taylor Cup, but the Chats had the last laugh as they pipped Cray to win the League.

Cray spent two years in the Greater London League, in 1964-65 and 1965-66. They won the championship in 1965-66 and the League Cup both years. Perhaps the greatest glory, however, was the hat-trick of Kent Amateur Cup wins. Bromley were again defeated, this time in a semi-final replay at Grassmeade watched by nearly 1,200, to earn the Wands a place in the two-legged final against Maidstone. In extra time

Cray Wanderers FC
1860 -2010

Founded 1860

in the second leg at Maidstone, Billy Smith belted home two tremendous left foot shots to give Cray victory by 3-2 on aggregate.

Team manager Arthur Barron certainly did the Wands proud during this period. His star players included Kent cap Ray Hutchins, a classy right-half, whilst alongside Ken Collishaw, Micky Thompson was a reliable goalscorer. The records show that Thompson scored exactly 100 goals for Cray; he was a fine header of the ball. Left winger Johnny Stevens, very effective when in harness with Collishaw and a confident penalty taker, was a great favourite with the crowd. He left Cray for Bromley, where he had an international trial, and then returned to Cray before moving on to Dartford for a long and successful stay. He died in 1985 at the very early age of 45. An interesting signing in 1965 was skilful permit professional Carlo Nastri, who had Football League experience with Crystal Palace.

Ted Saunders, a skilful right winger, and Micky Harrington, a bustling winger or inside forward, were both outstanding and had three separate spells for Cray. In 1964, Saunders scored what the *Kentish Times* called The Goal of the Century in a key league game with Herne Bay. In the last seconds, with the score at 2-2, he let fly from miles out on the right wing and brought the house down as the ball whistled past the 'keeper and into the net.

Mick Slater continued to make ground improvements at Grassmeade, to enhance his regular applications to join the Athenian League. A supporter, Mr Wimshurst, wrote to the local press with a tribute to Mick, 'Mr Slater has done more for local youth than any person in the district... he took Cray Wanderers from a poor ground behind Fordcroft to

their present ground where, through his drive, a covered stand for 1,500 people was erected, with two tiled modern dressing rooms, a free car park for 50 cars, a floodlit practice pitch and a licensed bar.'

Cray's groundsman was none other than the indomitable Shaver Harland, aged well into his seventies but still dedicated to the Wands. Amongst the many ex-players seen regularly at Grassmeade supporting Cray, the oldest was Lionel Jordan from the pre-1900 era, aged over 90 when he died in 1969. Mr Nicholls was a great stalwart on the committee, with more than 40 years service, and John Darrington was another enthusiastic servant. Mention should also be made of the club's reserve team, which enjoyed a number of successes in the 1950s and early 1960s, culminating in the winning of the Kent Intermediate Cup in 1965-66.

Cray made a major policy change in 1966-67 when they joined the Metropolitan League, playing as an amateur club in a mainly professional competition. Mick Slater was tired of receiving the cold shoulder from the Athenian League and decided that the Wands might fare better in an environment that was more akin to the Southern League.

Cray served up some attractive and memorable football during their five years in the Met. League. Particularly exciting were the encounters with the Arsenal, Spurs and West Ham A

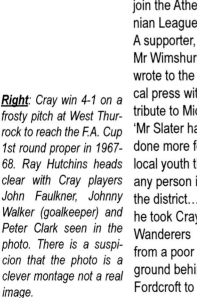

Right: Cray win 4-1 on a frosty pitch at West Thurrock to reach the F.A. Cup 1st round proper in 1967-68. Ray Hutchins heads clear with Cray players John Faulkner, Johnny Walker (goalkeeper) and Peter Clark seen in the photo. There is a suspicion that the photo is a clever montage not a real image.

**Cray Wanderers FC
1860 -2010**

Left: Drama at Grass-meade in the F.A. Amateur Cup 3rd round (last 16) in 1967-68. Barry Diggins is denied a goal as Cray draw 0-0 versus Barking.

team, when budding stars like Charlie George and Trevor Brooking played against the Wands. Cray also played the reserve sides of leading Southern League clubs like Chelmsford and Wimbledon, whilst their games against Met. Police allowed their intrepid match reporter, Ernie Ogilvie (E.B.O. of the *Kentish Times*) to indulge in some of his characteristic humour, 'Ron Wissenden put the ball into the net for Cray off a Graham Waghorn cross which the entire C.I.D. are still looking for!'

The Met. League was undoubtedly the strongest that Cray had played in after the war. They made a dreadful start to the 1966-67 season, suffering a string of heavy defeats, mainly away from home. After a 9-0 drubbing at Bury Town the day after Boxing Day, Mick Slater actually sent in Cray's resignation from the league, but results improved significantly from January onwards, as centre-forward Barry Diggins hit form. Diggins attracted plenty of interest from professional clubs, and was watched by an England amateur international selector. He had a run of scoring in nine out of ten games and notched 42 in total for the season.

A 1-0 victory at Folkestone in the Kent Senior Cup, thanks to a last-minute Billy Thornton goal, was an excellent result – Cray's first ever win over a Southern League Premier Division side.

Left: There were more F.A. Amateur Cup heroics from the 1968-69 team that beat Lewes and Torpoint before losing to the holders Leytonstone after a replay. Back row (L to R): John Darrington (Secretary), Norman Golding (Manager), John Faulkner, Alan Bishop, Tex Wiltshire, Ian Hook, Mick Gauntlett, Alan Howe, Peter Clark, Arthur Styles (Trainer). Front row: Norman Lawrence, Danny McDermott, John Dorey, Colin McGannon, John Mears.

Cray Wanderers FC 1860 -2010

Below: The team in 1970-71. Back row (L to R): Unknown, Haydn Diggins (Trainer), Jack Payne (Manager), Bobby Baker, Colin McGannon, Keith Beerling, Ray Woolley, John Dorey, Graham Waghorn, Alan Howe, Terry Smith, John Keith. Front row: Dave le Grice, Bobby Etherington, Junior Crooks, Peter Deadman, Trevor Ford, Keith Wellham.

The Wands eventually finished 9th in the league and won the shield for the highest placed amateur club, which they retained the following year.

Wembley fever came to Cray for the first time in 1967-68. Cray's best run (at that time) in the F.A. Cup took them to the 3rd qualifying round where they lost 1-0 at Dagenham. This proved to be a dress rehearsal for their best ever F.A. Amateur Cup run.

The Wands battled through five qualifying rounds, the highlight being a 6-1 demolition of old rivals Herne Bay at Grassmeade when the stylish Tex Wiltshire, a great striker of a dead ball, scored a hat-trick. In the 1st round proper, Eastbourne were brushed aside 4-1, earning Cray a trip to top Athenian League side Hayes. Some stout defending and a fine display by goalkeeper Johnny Walker kept the scoresheet goalless, before Cray produced a shock win in the replay, an own goal past goalkeeper Graham Roope (a Surrey and England cricketer) settling the tie. Now in the last sixteen, Cray entertained

Barking the following week. A crowd of over 2,000 saw Cray miss several chances in a 0-0 draw, and they lost the replay 2-0.

Cray again had a thrilling time in the F.A. Amateur Cup in 1968-69. A very long journey to Torpoint, on the borders of Devon and Cornwall, brought a 3-1 win in the 1st round, earning a 2nd round home tie against mighty Leytonstone, the cup holders. The 2-2 draw with Leytonstone (attendance 2,160) was undoubtedly the finest game ever seen at Grassmeade. John Faulkner gave the Wands a 46th minute lead and, although the visitors struck back with two quick goals, Cray deserved their sensational equaliser when Norman Lawrence sent in a spectacular diving header from Wiltshire's cross. The Stones won a hard-fought replay 2-0.

Cray's manager, Norman Golding, ex-QPR, had Peter Clark and Alan Howe as a splendid and long-serving partnership at full back, while Johnny Walker and Ian Hook played brilliantly

in goal. The Wands had an exceptionally good half-back line of the experienced Hutchins and Dorey, along with young Faulkner who went on to Sutton United and was signed by Don Revie for Leeds United in 1971. After four first team games there, he went to Luton Town and played two hundred and nine games for them in the Football League appearances.

Ground problems resurface

After this breathless burst of excitement, the mood changed quite quickly at Grassmeade. The 1969-70 season was very poor, the most memorable result being Cray's shock home defeat in the semi-final of the Kent Amateur Cup to complete outsiders Eccles F.C.

Jack Payne took over as manager and enjoyed success in 1970-71 when the Wands finished 4th in the Met League and won the League Cup, defeating Bletchley 4-1 in the two-legged final. A 3-1 Kent Senior Cup victory against Maidstone was also a pleasing result. Graham Waghorn was the most consistent goalscorer, well supported by Ron Wissenden. There was sadness, though, when popular Keith Welham, who had recently scored a hat-trick in a league game against Bletchley, collapsed and died after a training run.

During the course of the 1970-71 season, Cray's future was suddenly plunged into uncertainty. Not only was it announced that the Met. League was folding, mainly due to the exodus of some clubs into the Southern League, but worse still, St Philomena's Convent, the owners of Grassmeade, announced they were selling the land for housebuilding. The Wands would have to leave their well-appointed ground – a devastating blow at a time when the club otherwise seemed to be progressing extremely well, and might have been considered in line to move up at last to the Athenian League or even the Southern.

There followed several months of agonising over a possible new ground. For a while, open land at Brow Crescent, not far from Grassmeade, offered a possible site, but it had numerous drawbacks. There was great relief when Mick Slater's discussions with Sidcup Conservative Club led to the offer of a ground at Oxford Road, off Sidcup Hill between Footscray and Sidcup High Streets. Moreover, Cray managed to hold on to Grassmeade until the end of 1972-73, allowing precious time to upgrade the facilities at Oxford Road. But one wonders how all the worry, as well as a busy working life managing Bryant's woodyard in Orpington, may have contributed to Mick's death, shortly after the move was completed.

Mick also had to contend with a widely-publicised drama when Jack Payne and all the players walked out on the Wands midway through the 1971-72 season. Cray had been forced to enter the new Met London League (an amalgamation of the Greater London and what little was left of the Metropolitan League), but the players understandably felt this was a downgrade in status, and they departed in search of clubs who played in a higher standard of football. Cray sadly bade farewell to popular players like John Dorey, Colin McGannon and Trevor Ford. Caretaker manager Jim Paris came in and raised a scratch side who fulfilled Cray's remaining fixtures, winning one game against Eton Manor but losing all the rest.

The big walkout got Cray's name on to the sports page of some of the national newspapers in 1971-72. There was also a mention in some of the dailies of a strange

Left: Skilful midfielder Ron Wissenden scores for Cray in 1970-71.

**Cray Wanderers FC
1860 -2010**

incident during Epping Town's 1-0 win against Cray. Epping's player-manager was sent off twice during the game! – firstly from the field, and later from the dug-out!

For 1972-73, the last season at Grassmeade, Cray brought in an ambitious young manager, Johnny Biddle. As though to signify the end of an era, the club kit was changed back to amber shirts and black shorts.

Biddle and several of his players had been together at junior clubs, most recently Vokins and 279 Chislehurst. They were inexperienced in senior football but they settled in well to finish a creditable 4th in the Met London League. The team was nicknamed Biddle's Battlers, a reference to their robust style of play, as well as excellent team spirit.

Biddle and his team also had to cope with a new offside law in their early season Met London League matches. The F.A. asked Cray and the other member clubs to try out a proposed new change where offside would only apply if the offending player was inside the penalty area. The experiment was not a success – the feedback from Cray and the other Met London League clubs was so negative that the F.A. soon abandoned the trial.

Many of Biddle's players had careers with Cray that spanned several spells. These included top scorers Terry Smart and John Duffy, winger Pat

Carey, and Dave Fiander and Gerry Collier, who could play almost anywhere. Goalkeeper Dave Jackson became a long-serving member of the club's committee after he retired from playing.

An exciting game at Grassmeade saw Jackson make a flying save from a penalty-kick in the final minutes to seal a 1-0 win for Cray against East Ham. But the last game ever played at a much-loved ground was a low-key 1-0 defeat to Willesden.

Right: A dramatic photo of Trevor Ford getting to the ball just in front of Graham Waghorn to head a goal in a 2-0 win versus West Ham 'A' in 1970-71.

Chapter 4 – Oxford Road: 'a well-darned sock'

Biddle's Battlers deliver the double

Cray's enforced departure from Grassmeade must have brought back painful memories for their oldest supporters who recalled the turmoil the previous time the club had been forced to move from St Mary Cray to Footscray, following the loss of Fordcroft in 1936. The strength of the committee dwindled as some saw this as the end of the road for Cray but Mick Slater and the remaining stalwarts ensured that the Wands made a successful move.

The ground at Oxford Road was brought up to the required standard as the volunteers erected a pavilion and dressing rooms. This was intended as a temporary base for Cray whilst a more permanent home was sought. Suitable land in Rectory Lane, Footscray, was found and was leased from Morphy Richards Ltd at a peppercorn rent, but a lack of financial resources meant that the club had to negotiate an extension to the short lease they had originally accepted at Oxford Road.

Johnny Biddle and the bulk of his squad made the move to the new ground; the first match resulted in a 3-1 victory over Swanley. The gate was a modest 200, smaller than would have been expected at Grassmeade. Cray again finished 4th in the Met. London League in 1973-74, but showed signs of maturing into a powerful team. Captain Phil Emblen was commanding at the back, whilst winger Paul McCarthy had tremendous pace and inspired Cray to an excellent 4-2 win at Southern League Ramsgate in the Kent Senior Cup.

Over the season, Biddle strengthened the side, acquiring the combative Scott brothers, John and Bob, and big strikers Paul Martin and Phil Lawrence. But the prize signing turned out to be that of Davy Waight, who was spotted playing five-a-sides. Waight was an immensely skilful midfield player, almost impossible to dispossess, with a superb eye for goal. He netted a total of 90 in three spells with Cray.

There was a big blow for the club in April 1974, when it was announced that Mick Slater had died, after a short illness. Secretary Micky Hunt said in a tribute in the programme 'No-one could have done more for any club than Mick, known everywhere as 'Mr Cray Wanderers.' He always did more than his share, building Grassmeade to what it was… only with his drive and experience has it been possible to develop the ground and facilities here at Oxford Rd. Mick is someone we will never be able to replace.'

When Cray won the end of season Harry Sunderland Memorial Trophy, beating Eton Manor 2-1 in the final, John Biddle held up the shield and said, on behalf of all Cray's supporters, 'This is for Micky Slater.'

It was in the 1974-75 season that Biddle's patient team-building paid off. The Wands were virtually unstoppable as defences could find no answer to the power and pace of Lawrence, Martin and McCarthy (who all scored over 20 goals) and the tricky skills of Waight, who notched 39. Opposition from better leagues found Cray's direct approach too hot to handle as well. The famous Walthamstow Avenue were defeated 2-0 in the F.A. Cup before a Sutton United side packed with amateur internationals won 5-1 in front of an

Below: One of the first photos of the Wands in action at Oxford Road, showing the original dressing rooms that were destroyed by fire. Tony Smith watches Cray winger Paul McCarthy run at the BROB Barnet defence in a 1973-74 Met London League game.

Cray Wanderers FC 1860 -2010

Founded 1860

Oxford Road crowd of 700. Their fellow Isthmian Leaguers, St Albans City and Barking, were defeated in the London Senior Cup, but this cup run was soured when 'keeper Mal Sutton broke his leg in the next round against Hitchin.

The season ended with a run of 29 unbeaten games that took Cray to a league and cup double. A record 170 goals were scored over the season. The Wands set off for a summer tournament in Holland (which they won) in buoyant mood. They had come through the tremendous upheaval of losing their ground remarkably well and seemed ready to take the newly-formed London Spartan League by storm. All appeared rosy, but the euphoria was broken by a double setback.

Jimmy Wakeling rebuilds

Johnny Biddle was hankering after a new challenge and, when offered the manager's post at Bromley, he accepted, taking nearly all of his Cray squad with him. The Wands appointed Jimmy Wakeling as their new boss. He had to begin the 1975-76 season with something of a scratch squad that included only one of the previous year's team but, as the season wore on, he was able to call on many of the men who had been to Bromley, as they drifted back to Cray; by the end of the year seven of them were back in the amber and black.

The campaign had hardly started when, on August Bank Holiday Monday, the club was rocked again, as the Oxford Road pavilion and dressing rooms were burned to the ground. Team kits and many historic photos were lost and temporary accommodation had to be used for much of the season, whilst a sturdier brick-built replacement was constructed. Work also began on the build-

Right: "Biddle's Battlers" end a record-breaking season as Met London League champions and League Cup winners. Back row (L to R): Johnny Biddle, Simon Emblen, Bobby Scott, Steve Pateman, Mal Sutton, Paul Martin, John Scott, Paul McCarthy, Keith Lawrence. Front row: Terry Smith, Phil Lawrence, Dave Waight, Phil Emblen, Dave Prountzos, Gerry Collier, Terry Smart. Photo: Trevor Mulligan.

ing of the pitch-side stand, which was terraced for about half its length, but left unfinished.

In the circumstances, it was scarcely surprising that Cray made little impact on the new league, finishing in mid-ta-

ble. They were able to look back, though, on one remarkable performance. In January the Wands travelled to unbeaten league leaders, Bracknell Town, with little expectation of success, and returned with a 5-0 victory, leading scorer Jimmy Crombie scoring twice. At the end of the season, Cray won the Harry Sunderland Shield again, winning 2-1 at Chalfont St Peter in the final, with Waight, who had returned from Hayes Lane a few weeks earlier, scoring twice.

Wakeling strengthened the side considerably for the 1976-77 season. Former favourite, Colin McGannon, returned, whilst defender Graham Taylor and speedy striker Steve Greenway proved shrewd signings. With Waight back to his best form (he top scored with 24 goals), Cray were again a strong force. The early season focus was on the F.A. Cup. After beating Erith in a replay, Cray were drawn at home to Maidstone United, then very much the 'giants' from the Southern League Premier Division, who boasted a squad of experienced, and expensive, players.

The B.B.C. local radio reported 'Maidstone were reckoned to be certain of progressing in the F.A. Cup at the expense of Cray Wanderers, but giant-killing acts are what the cup is all about and it was a case of 'Happy Wanderers' as they knocked the 'Stones out 2-1.'

A crowd of 719 saw Crombie and Brian Fitzpatrick net the vital goals in the second half. After the game, Jimmy Wakeling made the classic comment 'In my dreams last week I played the game 100 times, and this is the first time we have won!'

The victory earned Cray another home tie against, of all clubs, Bromley. The match generated enormous local interest, and the press con-

centrated on Biddle's personal situation, facing his former club and several of his former players. In the event, it was two ex-Cray players, Duffy and McCarthy, who got the goals in Bromley's 2-0 win, and spared Biddle's blushes.

***Left**: A controversial moment in the Cray v Bromley F.A. Cup 3QR tie at Oxford Road in 1976-77. The Wands thought they had taken the lead, but to their annoyance the referee had blown his whistle to give Cray a free-kick instead for a foul on Pat Carey.*
Photo: Tony Brown

The cup-ties meant Cray had fallen a long way behind in their league fixtures, but they steadily picked up points. Aided by their strong defence that conceded a record low total of goals, they drew level with leaders Alma Swanley and then beat them 4-1 as they took the London Spartan League Championship.

Cray retained the title in 1977-78, with their team boosted by Gary and Glen Cooper from Erith & Belvedere and Dermot Trainor, who pulled the strings in midfield alongside Waight. The star of the season was a powerful striker named Butch Dunn, who netted 32 goals at an average of exactly a goal a game. Dunn was the complete centre forward, strong in the air with clever ball-playing skills for a big man. His goals were the key factor in Cray retaining the league championship. The main challengers, Alma Swanley and Banstead, were both defeated during April and the title was secured with a 5-2 win at Farnham Town, in a game when the Wands were reduced to ten men with the score at 2-2, and Dunn scored a hat-trick.

There were celebrations, too, for the Cray reserve team, who won their section of the London Spartan League.

Back to the Kent League... & Vase adventures

Off the field, this was an important time as Cray received planning permission for the new ground in Rectory Lane. They also decided to leave the London Spartan League, which was rapidly losing well-equipped teams to higher leagues, and re-joined the Kent League. This was another echo of events in the 1930s, when a similar decision had been made at Fordcroft.

CRAY WANDERERS 2,
FARNHAM TOWN 1

FOR THE second time in three seasons Cray Wanderers are London Spartan League Champions. They finally grabbed the two points they needed to take the title when they overcame Farnham in a nailbiting clash at Oxford Road

With the tension showing Cray were forced to wait until three minutes from time before Steve Greenway nipped in to nod home the winner.

Earlier, they had hit the woodwork twice and missed a penalty—but those misfortunes were quickly forgotten as the celebrations greeted the final whistle.

***Left**: Celebrations at Oxford Road after winning the London Spartan League in 1976-77.*

**Cray Wanderers FC
1860 -2010**

Once again, the Wands lost their manager as they changed leagues. Bobby Sustins, an assured defender, took over as player-manager, but most of the previous season's squad left the club. Waight, Trainor and Dunn all went to Bromley. Dunn scored an astonishing 84 goals in his first two seasons at Hayes Lane, as Bromley were promoted to the Isthmian League Premier Division.

Sustins' makeshift team (twice they had no goalkeeper) made a disastrous start, winning only one game in nine. Cray failed to attract good players and Sustins was quickly replaced by Albert Dorey, an ex-player from the 1960s.

Right: A thrilling title showdown against Banstead in 1977-78. Two weeks after this vital 2-1 win Cray were the London Spartan League champions again.

Below: Team photo 1977-78. Back row (L to R): Jimmy Wakeling, Dermot Trainor, John Scott, Brian Fitzgerald, John Cox, Bob Hawkes, Glen Cooper, Steve Greenway, Albert Dorey, Butch Dunn. Front row: Dave Waight, Billy Parry, Gerry Collier, Pat Carey, Bobby Sustins.

THEY'RE HAPPY WANDERERS

CRAY WANDERERS 2, BANSTEAD 1

IT WAS blatantly obvious at Oxford Road last Saturday just why Cray and Banstead have forced the pace in the London Spartan League this season. In a championship decider which lived up to every expectation the Surrey side proved they are well equipped to deal with any slip their rivals might make during the run-in.

By Dave Powell

Results hardly improved and the Wands' problems deepened as they found themselves in disciplinary trouble.

Over the course of the year, nine different players were sent off, several of them experienced men who had returned to help the club out in this difficult season. In one game with Erith, four players got their marching orders and a supporter assaulted the referee. Cray faced a total ban from football, but escaped with a severe reprimand. Dorey quit just before the end of the season and Alan Williams looked after the team for the remaining matches. The Wands finished a miserable year only five places off the bottom.

Kent League & F.A. Vase excitement

The transformation brought about by a new manager the following season, 1979-80, was remarkable. Harry Richardson, who played briefly for Cray at Grassmeade, brought with him the experienced Wally Hill as coach and fans' favourite from the 1950s and 60s, John Stevens, as his assistant. They assembled a star-studded team that played, almost unchanged, through the entire season:
• Goalkeeper Steve Biggs had been Southern League Tonbridge's 'Player of the Year';
• Both full-backs were highly experienced: Alan Payne played for Dartford in the F.A. Trophy final at Wembley and Ken Edwards had a long career at Erith & Belvedere in the Athenian League;

• Andy Bushell, also ex-Erith, and Tony Pamphlett, who went on to play in the Football League with Maidstone, were the assured centre-backs;
• Midfielders Micky Kelly (an excellent penalty-taker) and Eddie Jones, who possessed a ferocious shot and was team captain, had League experience with Charlton and Millwall, whilst Don Butterfill (ex-Sutton United) followed in the footsteps of his father, Les, who played for Cray in the 1950s;
• Terry Elphick from Crockenhill was a powerful winger who supplied plenty of ammunition for two strikers with lots of Southern League experience: the silky-skilled Kevin Walsh and Richardson's 'pocket battleship', Alan Whitehead.

It came as no surprise when this accomplished side began to sweep all before them. They remained unbeaten in the league until April and defeated Isthmian Leaguers Farnborough in the F.A. Cup, but it was in the F.A. Vase, the successor to the F.A. Amateur Cup, that Cray really made a name for themselves.

The Wands were lucky enough to receive a record seven straight home draws and local interest mounted with each round as the prospect of the final at Wembley drew closer. Cray

Below: High drama at Oxford Road as Cray beat Newbury Town 1-0 in a pulsating 5th round F.A. Vase tie in the 1979/80 season.

Cray Wanderers FC 1860 -2010

__Right__:Goalkeeper Steve Biggs makes a lunge for the ball while Cray teammate Alan Whitehead is sent tumbling as Stamford push forward in the F.A. Vase match at Oxford Road. Keith Alexander is the tall Stamford player.

beat Newbury 1-0 to become the first Kent club to reach the quarter-finals, Kelly's penalty settling the issue in front of a ground record gate of 856. This brought Stamford to Oxford Road and an even bigger crowd of 1,523. Cray had their chances to win, but eventually succumbed to an extra-time goal, in a game marred by trouble amongst the spectators.

With their Wembley dream shattered, Cray's season ended sadly. Canterbury beat them 2-1 in the Kent Senior Trophy final. In the league the Wands had many games in hand on leaders Chatham but were, for a time, frustrated when the Chats objected to them using Erith's floodlights for midweek games, in order to reduce the backlog. After making up a deficit of 18 points (only 2 points for a win), Cray lost the deciding game 1-0 at Chatham and finished runners-up. The gate at this game, 1,002, was the highest in any Kent League game since the league's reformation in 1968.

Despite these heartbreaks, Richardson kept nine of his team for the 1980-81 season and managed to avoid the fixture congestion that had ultimately defeated Cray the year before. Once again, the F.A. Vase was a priority. This time, the Wands had to travel, beating Fisher, Southall and Great Yarmouth, before meeting Irthlingborough Diamonds in the last 16. After an exciting 0-0

draw at home, Cray, racked by injuries, crashed out 6-0 in the replay. However, the Wands were able to maintain their momentum and forged ahead of Chatham to take the league title they richly deserved, finishing with nine straight victories to win the Kent League for the second time, 79 years after their first championship.

At the end of the season, Richardson, Hill and Stevens announced that they would be leaving the club. With the Oxford Road ground totally unsuitable for promotion, they felt they had taken the Wands as far as they could. They had brought great honour to Cray Wanderers in their two seasons in charge. The quality of their football was summed up by Slade Green manager, Pat Meagan, midway through the 1980-81 season, 'Cray are different class – the Kent League might just as well give them the title now and start a new competition for the rest of us'.

__Below__: Kevin Walsh finds his path blocked by a determined Stamford defence.

**Cray Wanderers FC
1860 -2010**

Left: Alan Whitehead celebrates after Eddie Jones scores at Swanley Town in 1979-80.

The Payne and Gaydon eras - the search for a ground continues

Most of Richardson's squad dispersed as he left, though Alan Payne took over as player-manager and, several of his colleagues later returned for further spells at Cray over his five years in charge. After the excitement of their first eight seasons at Oxford Road, the 1980s were a much quieter period for the club on the field, as slow and delicate negotiations continued over the Rectory Lane project.

Indeed, in 1981-82 Payne had to operate with only the barebones of a squad. Micky Hanson, who holds the record for Southern League appearances for Bexley United, turned out for Cray in his final season before retiring, and Ken Edwards was again superb in defence, but a run of poor results around Christ-

mas dashed any title hopes. Neil Adams, one of several members of the Cray Valley Paper Mills club, who joined the Wands, will remember this season as special, though. He scored five goals in a 9-1 win over Kent Police. Meanwhile, in a 0-0 draw with Crockenhill, 'keeper Dave Jackson had the satisfaction of making a superb save to deny future Irish international Tony Cascarino.

Experienced campaigners such as Waight, Duffy and Dave Lucas (ex-Wimbledon) joined Cray the following year, but the side was never settled and the promise of a superb 5-2 victory at Southern League Hounslow was never fulfilled. Last gasp 3-2 defeats at Chesham (F.A. Cup) and Burnham (F.A. Vase) were particularly heart-breaking.

Below: Cray win the Kent League championship in 1980-81. Alan Payne receives the trophy and lines up afterwards with the team. Back row (L to R): Tony Pamphlett, Alan Payne, Mick Kelly, Don Butterfill, Kevin Walsh, Dermot Trainor, Glen Cooper, Dave Jackson. Front row: Dave Wadhams, Kenny Edwards, Geoff Parsons, Andy Bushell, Eddie Jones, Alan Whitehead.

**Cray Wanderers FC
1860 -2010**

*Right: The team in 1981-82. Back row (L to R): Dave Jackson, Steve Greenway, Glen Cooper, Kevin Walsh, Gary O'Neill, Micky North, Micky Hanson, Bobby Adams, Alan Payne.
Front row: Paul Sanham, Kenny Edwards, Martin Taylor, Neil Adams, Barry Fulker.*

The side drifted down to mid-table after Duffy, who had scored 16 goals to the turn of the year, sensationally quit football, believing he had been harshly treated by referees. He was not replaced until the closing weeks of the 1982-83 season, which saw the arrival of former Chester striker, Phil Williams, an experienced goalscorer with pace and great aerial ability. He was reported to be the club's first player to sign a contract and immediately settled into a goal-a-game routine. Meanwhile, Cray's reserve team won the championship of the South London Alliance, a competition the Wands' first team had played in during the Second World War.

Payne was able to re-sign Kevin Walsh for 1983-84 and also snapped up flying winger Peter Cappuccio from Crockenhill. Along with Williams, who scored 36 goals during the season, the Cray front-line had a powerful look to it. Dave Quirke, who made 230 League appearances for Gillingham, slotted into defence. Williams scored six in Cray's 10-1 victory over Ramsgate (both were records at the ground) but a run of only one win

in eight games over Christmas and the New Year put paid to the Wands' league championship ambitions. Nevertheless, 4th place was a good finishing position.

There were celebrations at the end of the season, though. Cappuccio starred in a tremendously exciting 4-3 League Cup final win over Sheppey, Walsh sweeping home his cross for the winner, after Cray's fine 'keeper, Gary O'Neill, had saved a penalty with the score at 3-3. Two days later, Cray took part in the national finals of the Thorn-EMI Floodlighting Competition at the Alexander Stadium in Birmingham. The Wands had qualified by being the highest scorers in league matches in their regional qualifying group. The prize of a set of floodlights would have been most welcome but, with Williams (whose goals had gained Cray a place in the finals) struggling with injury, the Wands made little impact.

Cray lost three key players to injury in the first game of the 1984-85 season and Williams was often far from fully fit, although he still managed a tally of 23 goals. Several players from the reserve side, including Alan White and Richard Palmer, were given their chance, but the Wands were never seriously in contention for the league title. Bromley gave them a 4-0 hiding in the F.A. Cup, but there were two good F.A. Vase victories over Isthmian League sides Horsham and Banstead; Cappuccio scored twice as Cray came from behind to beat Banstead.

*Right: Cray's end-of-season line-up in 1982-83. Back row (L to R): Dave Jackson, Paul Edgar, Gary O'Neill, Micky Wills, Richard Heselden, Kenny Edwards, Steve Greenway, Alan Payne.
Front row: Phil Williams, Alan Whitehead, Glen Cooper, Terry French, Neil Lawrence.*

In October 1985 the local press announced that Cray were on the brink of purchasing the Rectory Lane site and would develop it at the cost of £120,000. But it soon became clear that the loan repayments would be prohibitive and the plan was temporarily shelved. Meanwhile, the team had gone into serious decline. Williams broke his foot in the first game of the 1985-86 season and five-goal defeats at Canterbury (F.A. Cup), Southwick (F.A. Vase) and in the league at home to perennial strugglers Ramsgate made the autumn a depressing time for the dwindling band of supporters. Gates had fallen to an average of around 75 and they would stay at this level for the next 15 years.

shalton, Dulwich and Tooting, Gaydon brought some experienced faces to Cray. These included former Dartford defender Bobby Pittaway as skipper, and Colin Ford and Ian Crouch from Welling United. Ex-player Alan Walker took over as chairman and talk of developing the new ground began again.

Things did not improve and leading players Walsh and Cappuccio left. Despite moving to Erith in February, Cappuccio remained top scorer with 9 goals out of a miserable total of 43! Then, at Easter, Alan Payne resigned. It was a sad end to seven years of sterling service for the club. Reserve boss Trevor Willis took over as care-taker-manager and immediately conjured up four wins, which kept the Wands out of the re-election zone. Supporters voted Glen Cooper their Player of the Season for the second year running, only for him to leave for Greenwich Borough, who were Kent League champions for the next two years.

A new regime took over for the following season. Peter Gaydon was appointed the new manager. A well-known character in Isthmian League circles, having played as centre-half for Car-

Somewhat belatedly, the 125th anniversary of the club was celebrated with pre-season friendlies against Arsenal (1-5), Charlton (2-0) and Wimbledon (2-2). Former England captain, Gerry Francis, played for the Dons. The new-look side made a poor start, though, and it needed the arrival of new wingers Micky Paye, who had League experience for Charlton, and Paul Brown to revive Cray's fortunes. Just one defeat in fourteen games saw the Wands climb the table and they also made good headway in the Kent Senior Trophy. Long-serving midfielder Terry French scored the 1-0 winner in a tense semi-final against Whitstable.

The Trophy final against Southern League Cor-inthian at Dartford made for an exciting climax to the season, but one that ended in bitter disap-pointment. Cray soon took command and Paye

Above: Phil Collins eludes a Crockenhill defender at Wested Meadow in 1983-84.

Left: Goal celebrations during Cray's exciting 4-3 win against Shep-pey United in the Kent League Cup final at Sit-tingbourne in 1983-84. Don Butterfill and Phil Williams net the first two goals for Cray.

**Cray Wanderers FC
1860 -2010**

put them into the lead. As the game went into injury time, with the amber and black ribbons already attached to the cup and the Wands' supporters in carnival mood, Corinthian had a hopeful long-range shot and the ball sailed in for the equaliser. Despite a

battling performance from Cray, Corinthian ran out 3-2 winners in the replay at Sittingbourne.

Cray returned to the top half of the table in each of the following two seasons, without seriously threatening for the title. Highlights of the early part of 1987-88 included a 3-1 F.A.Cup win at Isthmian League Basildon (The Non-League Directory called this 'the result of the round'), an 8-0 win against Deal (Williams scored five) and a 2-1 win at champions Greenwich in the League Cup. But Greenwich got their revenge, hammering Cray 6-1 at Oxford Road on Boxing Day and this proved a turning point as the season fizzled out. A 2-1 defeat in the League Cup semi-final at Hythe put an end to any hopes of silverware, but Williams and Crouch could look back on a productive year, as they shared 50 goals. On his retirement from playing, Crouch took up refereeing and became a well-respected top local official.

This page: 'The Power of Phil': Phil Williams on the rampage. The awesome power of Phil's heading and shooting will be remembered by Cray supporters for a very long time.

Left: Cray take on Arsenal at Oxford Road to mark the Wands' 125th anniversary in 1985-86.

Ex-England Schools International Micky Pittaway joined the club in 1988-89, to play alongside his brother, Bobby. He scored in the second game, a 4-1 win against Kent Police, but more importantly, Phil Williams notched his 100th goal for the Wands in the same match. Otherwise, it was a mediocre start and Peter Gaydon re-shaped his side around a number of talented newcomers, including Jimmy Nunn, Tony Young, Kevin Langford and Danny Carlisle. Results improved and a great 2-1 victory over runaway league leaders, the mega-rich Hythe Town, took Cray into the Kent Senior Trophy semi-finals. But a last-minute defeat at Ramsgate left the Wands empty-handed.

Meanwhile, under Alan Walker's guidance, a very ambitious set of new plans for the Rectory Lane site had been drawn up. These envisaged a stadium fit for the 21st century, with two stands, floodlights, gymnasium and warden's accommodation. A new access road was to be constructed off Baugh Road, Footscray. Despite some local objections, Bexley Council planners gave the go-ahead in December 1989 and a bright new dawn for Cray Wanderers seemed finally about to begin.

It mattered little that the 1989-90 season was a dreadful time on the pitch. Cray suffered their heaviest defeat for 20 years (7-1 at Faversham) and finished third from bottom in the league, their worst position since 1950. Leading scorer was Brian Inglis (ex-Greenwich), one of the few consistent performers throughout the season.

Williams played his final game in April 1990. He had scored 126 goals since arriving at the club seven years earlier, the second-highest tally of goals recorded for the Wanderers. Nicknamed

Left: Have a Good Day, Cray!' Ian Crouch in action during the Kent Senior Trophy final at Dartford in 1986-87. But a late equaliser by Corinthian spoilt the day for the Wands.

Cray Wanderers FC 1860 -2010

'The Goal Machine', Phil was an immensely powerful striker, with a fierce turn of pace over ten yards. Not an especially tall man, he had tremendous spring. Photographs show him a huge distance above the ground as he leaped for headers, and they left his forehead like a rocket. He also had the goalscorer's poaching instinct, converting a high proportion of the chances that fell to him and he was always worrying defenders and goalkeepers. An example of this was in the Kent League Cup final in 1984. The Sheppey 'keeper was rolling the ball to the edge of his box before clearing upfield (the 'four-step' rule was in force then), only for a half-fit Phil to dart forward and toe-poke the ball between his legs for the cheekiest of goals!

The 1990-91 season opened with enormous optimism. Work was about to begin in the new stadium and Peter Gaydon was given a much-increased budget, with the aim, it seemed, of gaining quick promotion to the Southern League, playing at Rectory Lane the following year.

New signings included experienced 'keeper Gary Moseley, Tonbridge's former Charlton midfielder Tony Booth and Matt Norris, an exciting young striker from Dulwich. Three more ex-Tonbridge men – Mark Gillham, Dave Boyton and Paul Collins – provided a strong backbone for the side. Peter Cappuccio who, incidentally, had been best man at his school friend Tony Cascarino's

wedding, returned for his best season at the club, scoring 32 goals.

This powerful line-up soon proved very consistent. An early season defeat at Sittingbourne, who had similar plans to the Wands, preceded a run of 18 games without defeat. This included a very sweet league double over Tonbridge and a remarkable burst of scoring by Neil Missen, signed from Alma. He found the net in each of his first seven appearances for Cray.

Suddenly, in the early months of the New Year, things began to look much less rosy for the club. Deal Town ended the unbeaten run in the semi-final of the Kent Senior Trophy, winning 4-2 after Cray had led 2-0. This was followed by the dreadful news that due to the recession, Alan Walker's company were pulling out of all sponsorship. To their credit, the players battled on to the end of the season, finishing comfortably in second place, suffering only two defeats. This achievement was eclipsed, though, by Sittingbourne, who finished unbeaten as champions and duly entered the Southern League at their new stadium.

By contrast, Cray ended 1990-91 in turmoil. Gaydon accepted the manager's job at Isthmian League Croydon, all the players left and an administrative error meant the club were not entered for the F.A.Cup and Vase for the follow-

Right: The team in 1987-88. Back row (L to R): Alan White, Phil Williams, Ian Crouch, Bobby Pittaway, Alan Rogers, Dave Fisher, George Henning, Peter Gaydon. Front row: Robbie O'Brien, Danny Mace, Micky Paye, Dave Francis, Bobby Oaten.

Cray Wanderers FC
1860 -2010

Left: Cray v Sheppey in 1991.
Photo: Mike Floate

Left: Paul Collins scores against Sheppey.
Photo: Mike Floate

Below: Cray in 1989-90.

Cray Wanderers FC 1860 -2010

Founded 1860

Right: So near and yet so far in 1990-91. A few weeks after this dramatic game against Sitting-bourne at Oxford Road, the news broke that the proposed new ground at Rectory Lane was a shattered dream.

Below: Line-up in 1990-91 before a hard-fought 4-2 win versus Sangley Sports in the Kent Senior Trophy. Back row (L to R): Bill Lepage (Coach), Peter Cappuccio, Matt Norris, Dave Boyton, Gary Moseley, Dave Clarke, Paul Collins, Kevin Langford, Peter Gaydon (Manager). Front row: Tony Booth, Bob McKie, Micky Paye, Martin Johnson, Steve Daws, Mark Gillham.

ing season. To cap it all, the Kent League threatened to expel Cray if the Oxford Road ground, undeveloped for years because of the hoped-for move, was not improved within 12 months. As for the new stadium, other than fencing and site clearance, no work was ever started on the project, which was now clearly never going to happen. A dream, which had sustained the club for nearly fifteen years, had died an embarrassing and painful death.

More uncertainty

It was 'back to square one' for the Cray committee and they brought in Eddie Davies as the new manager. Davies had had some success as reserve and youth team boss at Fisher Athletic and from

Sitting target stuns Wands!

KEEPING politics out of sport is a maxim that Sidcup side Cray Wanderers would find it difficult to respect.

For the last 17 years, they've been the tenants of the local Conservative Association, whose headquarters in Oxford Road shield the ground from public notice.

At present, however, the little club which originated at St Mary Cray and claims to be the second oldest in the country — it was formed in 1860 — has plenty to shout about.

Their record of only one defeat in 20 matches had carried them to within sight of the summit of the Winstonlead Kent League and on Saturday they entertained the only team to beat them this season, leaders Sittingbourne, themselves without a loss in 24.

The result was a tidy little crowd of 350, four times the norm, and a closely fought contest that wouldn't have been out of place a few rungs up the non-League ladder.

Among the enthusiasts, remarkably, was former Millwall striker Tony Cascarino, who knows a thing or two about the Kent League, having once moved on from neighbouring Crockenhill in exchange for a set of tracksuits.

But football at this level is less about

**Cray Wanderers 1
Sittingbourne 1**
RICK EVERITT
at Oxford Road

the spectators and more about the dedicated officials that keep the team playing. In this respect, Cray is no different from 10,001 other little clubs that dot the map of Britain.

On Saturday, they were exemplified by chairman and physio Brian Faulkner, brother of Luton coach John, who was looking after the pennies in the most practical way by retrieving the ball whenever it strayed into the surrounding fields.

His reward came four minutes from the end of a first half in which the Brickies, as the visitors are apparently known, had briefly threatened to run riot.

Confusion

Playing down the inevitable slope, they contrived to miss four good chances in the opening quarter of an hour, the best of which was crashed against the bar by the unmarked Wayne Schweiso.

Cray, perhaps in the same state of confusion about the time of the kick-off as many of the crowd, took half an hour to find their feet.

But when they did, a Sittingbourne arm soon flapped inadvisedly at a loose

ball in the penalty area and referee Goodwin duly obliged.

So too did Peter Cappuccio, with a ferocious strike that made him joint leading scorer for the season with Matt Norris on 12 goals.

Yet as the evening gloom gathered, so too did the threat from Sittingbourne, prompting a tremendous save from former West Ham keeper Gary Moseley and anxious Wands manager Peter Gaydon to pace the touchline barking orders.

Ten minutes from time he leapt in premature celebration as ex-Dulwich striker Norris turned sharply on the edge of the box and hooked a match-winning strike past keeper Hough. But delight turned to exasperation at the raising of the linesman's flag.

Now Hemmings hit a post for the visitors, and worse was to follow.

As Sittingbourne mounted a final frantic assault, the ball flew across the goalmouth from the left, eluded every desperate defender's lunge and there was an ecstatic Gary Julians to poke it home from close range. There was barely time to kick off.

Momentarily crestfallen, the Wands officials trudged away in disappointment. But there's had been a memorable afternoon, and even now its outcome offered the promise of more to come.

Eleven points adrift in second place, they still retain four games in hand. Enthusiasm always did nurture optimism.

Even if they do make it, there will be no place for them in the Beazer Homes League while they remain at Oxford Road. But planning permission has been granted for a new 4,500-capacity ground less than half a mile away in Rectory Lane.

That, however, must await a fall in interest rates. And in one sense at least, they seem likley to remain high at Cray for some time yet.

Cray Wanderers: Moseley, Langford, Booth, Missen, Boyton, Johnson, Paye, Clark, Gillham, Cappuccio, Norris. Subs (not used) Dalton, Draper.

that source came the bulk of the squad that he initially brought to Oxford Road. He also helped the club to find sufficient financial support and advertising revenue to keep the wolf from the door.

The new side adapted quite well to Kent League football and held their own for the first half of the 1991-92 season. Leading scorer Craig Hanlon got four goals in a 5-2 win at Crockenhill and wingers Paul Smith and Arron Dodds, along with Robert Welch in defence, all looked promising.

Left: Cray fans see a shot saved in the KST semi final against Deal. Photo: Mike Floate

Some interesting temporary signings of more experienced men were made, including Danny Esquilant, who had been on Arsenal's books, and Clive Gartell and Barry Blackman, who had Isthmian League experience.

Then, without warning, the lights well and truly went out on the Wands after Christmas. Nine games in a row were lost and only six points were added from the last 20 games, which left Cray just one point above the relegation zone. By contrast, Cray's youth team, playing in the Kent Youth League for the first time, performed extremely well and reached the League Cup final.

Off the pitch, the club managed to retain Kent League status, by at long last completing construction of the stand, with 100 seats from Charlton's Valley. It must have been one of football's longest building projects, as it had been started 16 years earlier!

The following season (1992-93) began with four defeats (which made it 23 in 25 games) but the tide turned dramatically with an 8-0 victory at Kent Police. New signing Frank Murphy scored a hat-trick. Murphy, who had League experience for Barnet, left to play for Kettering in the Conference shortly after, but returned for a few games at the end of the season, when Cray's form improved again. A classy striker, he later

Left: Pat Brown makes a great save in the KST semi final against Deal. Photo: Mike Floate

**Cray Wanderers FC
1860 -2010**

became a top non-league manager. Also in the Kent Police game, a centre-forward of the more direct variety, Phil Collins, scored his first goal for the club. He went on to be top scorer with 27.

Cray's league form remained poor, but the team put together some useful cup runs. Victories over Chichester, Oakwood and Merstham put the Wands into the last 64 of the F.A. Vase, only to lose disappointingly 2-3 at home to Tring Town. They also reached the semi-final of the London Senior Cup (now a lower-status competition), losing at Hanwell Town after extra-time, but it was in the Kent Senior Trophy that it seemed the Wands' 'name was on the cup.'

In the first round at Midland Bank, Cray won 2-0 as physio Brian Mayo hit the headlines; he per-formed life-saving first aid on an opposing player who had swallowed his tongue. A thrilling 4-3 victory at Folkestone Invicta was followed by Cray's first win in a penalty shoot-out, in the quarter-final replay at Thamesmead. When 'keeper Pat Brown saved the vital spot-kick, he was duly submerged under his jubilant team-mates! The semi-final saw Cray lead Deal 2-1 in injury time, only for the visitors to equalise. Fortunately, Ian Jenkins, playing one of his first games for the club, struck an extra-time winner for the Wands. Remarkably, at this point in the season, Cray had won nine cup-ties but only three league games.

They were still bottom of the league when they travelled to Gillingham to play Whitstable in Trophy final, a repeat of the Kent Amateur Cup final 64 years earlier.

Misery as Town let silverware slip away again

Kent Senior Trophy final

Whitstable 0 Cray 1

by Stephen Constable

IT WAS hard to believe. Not that Whitstable could lose, yet again, in a cup final, but that they could lose so meekly.

The frustration of Town's fourth final defeat in four years, against the side bottom of the Winstonlead Kent League, was compounded by the knowledge that they could, and should, have done so much better.

Faced with tricky selection decisions, manager Peter Merritt understandably plumped for experience, leaving the promising but relatively unproven talents of Barry Morgan and Graeme Savage on the bench.

But the Whitstable contingent, the larger among more than 600 spectators at Gillingham's Priestfield Stadium on Saturday, were baffled as John Crabbe, Sammy Spence, Peter Venn and Wayne Draper were first out-fought in the opening midfield skirmishes, then, increasingly, bypassed as their own defenders sought to ease the pressure with long punts forward.

In the first half Gary Pullen, who, like Spence, had been battling against fitness problems in the build-up to the match, stayed wide on the right, while Rashid Short struggled vainly against the Cray defence.

After the interval Whitstable took control, but Cray keeper Pat Brown had only one difficult save to make.

And when versatile Sam Wright, overcoming his own injury worries to play at right back, powered home a header from Arron Dodds' corner in the 75th minute, it seemed no more than Cray really deserved.

The alarms were ringing in the second minute when Nick Day, Town's man-of-the-first-half, had to race from his goal to punch the ball away from Cray's dangerman, the muscular Phil Collins.

In the 10th minute Pullen's pass to Short was cut out by Robert Welch, and Spence put the rebound wide.

Day was kept busy dealing with crosses and long balls into his area, and, though Town threatened when Crabbe's quick free-kick put Venn clear, Pullen was too far behind play to reach the pass across goal.

Short missed with his head from Spence's centre, but Day had to kick clear from Cray's stand-in skipper Ian Jenkins after Collins had again disrupted the defence.

Pullen shot tamely off-target on the half-hour, but six minutes from half-time Day denied Cray with an astonishing double save.

First he parried Collins' point-blank drive, and somehow recovered to push the ball away from Jenkins, standing almost on the goal-line.

The second half began with Pullen and Venn immediately pushing forward and, from a 51st-minute free kick, Dave Linstrem's header was easily taken by Brown.

Seven minutes later Venn broke up a Cray attack, and Crabbe's through ball was chased by Pullen and won by Short, whose shot was held by Brown, diving to his left.

Pullen opened the defence again in the 66th minute with a clever turn and fine pass to Short, who shot into the side netting.

Then Pullen's shot from a corner was blocked and skipper Geoff Record, in his 201st appearance for the club, put the rebound wide.

The match finally turned on two decisive interventions by Wright, who first slid the ball away for a corner after Pullen had beaten Brown to a through pass.

Within five minutes Wright was heading the ball past Day at the other end, and suddenly Cray were back on top.

Barry Gethin made a saving tackle to deny Craig Hanlon a chance, and Dave Woodgate and Hanlon put headers wide from good positions.

Savage and Morgan replaced Venn and Draper, but by then the awful inevitability of Whitstable's disappointment was all too clear.

Whitstable: Day, Gethin, Godden, Record, Linstrem, Draper (sub, Morgan 79 min), Crabbe, Spence, Pullen, Venn (sub, Savage 79 min), Short.

Cray: Brown, Wright, Partridge, Rothery, Allwright, Welch, Woodgate, Jenkins, Collins, Hanlon, Dodds. Subs. Down, Ansah.

Right: Sam Wright's goal brings the Kent Senior Trophy to Cray in 1992-93.

This time Cray were the underdogs, but the 612 spectators saw Sam Wright head a late winner for the Wands to take the club's only silverware of the 1990s. This success had a dramatic effect on Cray's league form. They won six of their last eight league games (earning as many points as they had in the previous 36 games!) and comfortably avoided the bottom two.

Any hopes that Eddie Davies could build on this success soon evaporated. Collins and Hanlon both suffered serious injuries in the 1993-94 pre-season matches and Cray's form in the first three months of the season was poor.

The Cray team in jubilant form. Photo: Mike Floate.

Magic Wands

Cray Wanderers cast a spell on Mike Floate at the recent Kent Senior Trophy Final.

ray Wanderers' pre-war forward Jumbo Collins used to greet defeats for his former club by commenting "it looks like I'll have to get the old boots out again."

Sadly, Jumbo died last Autumn as Cray made one of the worst starts to a season in their 133 year history. By Easter things were no better – with 32 games played Cray were firmly rooted at the foot of the Winstonlead Kent League with just 22 points.

Cup games proved to be an altogether different matter as the club reached the last 64 of the FA Vase and only bowed out of the London Senior Cup after extra-time in the semi-final. In the Kent Senior Trophy semi-final Cray took on a Deal team with over 100 league goals to their credit, only to reduce the normally potent forwards to arguing amongst themselves as Cray survived a last minute equaliser to win convincingly in extra-time.

Cray manager, Eddy Davies, was at a loss to explain his team's cup form; "if I knew, I'd be worth a fortune. But we have done well in all of the cups. It's been the same players but they have just played with a bit more grit and determination."

The final tie was to be an attractive fixture against Whitstable at Gillingham's Priestfield Stadium. Among the excellent turnout of Cray fans was Gordon Creasey known as "Pop" to all at the club and, at the age

Cray's Arren Dodds finds a way past the Whitstable midfield. Photo: Mike Floate.

of 83, the proud owner of a free pass to all Cray games until the turn of the century. Pop first saw Cray play at the age of 10 at the old Fordcroft ground in St Mary Cray and went on to hold many posts within the club over the years. "I do look forward to my football and they are nice officials at the club now. They look after me so well, take me round – especially the secretary, Kerry Phillips. The team are not that bad but there has been too much chopping and changing. I think they will improve next year."

The team are not a typical bottom-of-the-table outfit, despite the budget available to the manager. Cray have never owned their own ground and lack the vital source of income that a bar and clubhouse can be. Cray's former chairman had intended to move to a purpose-built ground, plans for which were published locally, and would have given the club the best facilities in the area. However, two years ago it was obvious that the move was off and considerable costly work was needed to be done on the ground in order to stay in the Kent League. The stand that was started and left unfinished on their arrival at Oxford Road 20 years ago was eventually completed. It must surely be the longest construction job ever at any ground.

Looking ahead to the final Eddy Davies was realistic; "we are the underdogs, but we are not a bad side – we never get walloped. If you said to me 'do you want the cup or nine points?' I'd take the points."

Eddy planned to sit back and enjoy the game leaving the shouting to his assistant. John Dunbar was hopeful of seeing a good game; "we want to play well as we try to play football and not just hump it about. We must have a chance as we always seem to raise our games in the cups."

The match itself was a tense struggle between two evenly matched sides and the 612 fans made for a great atmosphere as they urged their sides on. With 72 minutes gone Cray won a rare corner and, with the keeper coming out too far, defender Sam Wright got up to score with an unstoppable header. The defence then produced a heroic display to keep Whitstable out in the dying minutes until, at last, the club could celebrate winning their first trophy in nine years.

A long season behind them, Cray could justifiably feel proud of a famous victory. With the spirit in the current squad it is unlikely that they will need the services of any veterans – though they will always be well looked after as spectators! ■

Gordon Creasey - "Pop" - shows off the trophy. Photo: Mike Floate.

Cray Wanderers Fact File

Formed:	1860
Address:	Oxford Road, Sidcup, Kent
Manager:	Eddy Davies
Colours:	Amber/Black
Nickname:	The Wands
Record attend':	1,523 versus Stamford, FA Vase 6th round 1980
Notable first:	First amateur club with floodlights – 1953
Notable second:	Second oldest club in the world
Honours:	12 League Championships, 19 Cup Final Victories

Five Year Record:
Winstonlead Kent League

	P	W	D	L	F	A	Pts	Pos
1987-88	36	16	7	13	72	51	55	7th
1988-89	38	19	7	12	67	53	64	7th
1989-90	38	7	11	20	48	74	32	18th
1990-91	40	27	11	2	91	33	92	2nd
1991-92	40	8	7	25	38	84	31	18th

JIII NLFT 19

__Left__: Mike Floate , the editor of this book, profiled the Wands in this article published in 'Non-League Football Today' in 1993.

Cray Wanderers FC
1860 -2010

Top left: Dave Woodgate.

Top right: Dave Woodgate and Sam Wright press the Whitstable goal.

Far right: Aaron Dodds.

Right: Cray skipper Ian Jenkins receives the Kent Senior Trophy.

Right: Cray line up for a team photo before the match.

All photos on this page: Mike Floate

Davies, who certainly had an ability to persuade a succession of interesting recruits to join the club (but often for very short periods), made some good new signings, including Gary Fiore (Bromley), Paul Burke (Welling) and Sierra Leonean Saidu Kanu.

This led to an improvement, notably a good performance in a 3-1 defeat at Conference club Welling in the Kent Senior Cup. As Senior Trophy holders, Cray were given entry into the county's top competition, after a gap of 20 years. By the end of the season, though, the Wands were back in the bottom five. They were well and truly upstaged by the re-born Dartford club, who Cray's committee had helped to get back on their feet by allowing them to ground-share at Oxford Road for this season. The Darts repaid the compliment by attracting gates five times bigger than their hosts, finishing sixth in the league and beating Cray three times!

Left: Dave Woodgate slides the ball under the Crocks 'keeper Kieran Murray in the 6-0 home win in the last game of 1992/3.

The first game of 1994-95 was a taste of things to come. Cray lost 3-0 at home to Sheppey with Phil Collins getting a hat-trick against his former club. Despite more impressive signings, including former Charlton striker Leroy Ambrose and Erith's Jamie Kempster, things quickly deteriorated. There were four five-goal defeats in a dozen games.

Below: Robert Welch battles with Crocks forward Gary Andrews in the last game of 1992/3. Both photos on this page: Mike Floate

Cray Wanderers FC
1860 -2010

Founded 1860

When perpetual whipping-boys Kent Police won 1-0 at Oxford Road in October, in front of a 'crowd' of just 32 spectators, it was clearly time for a change.

Davies, who had struggled manfully against the odds, resigned, along with chairman Bob Dell, and were replaced immediately by Alan Whitehead as manager and, perhaps the club's greatest ever 'signing', Gary Hillman as chairman.

Whitehead, who had briefly managed the Cray reserve side after his playing career ended, moved from the hot-seat at Crockenhill. He brought a number of players with him from Wested, notably the Twiner brothers, Paul and Mark, and Gary Wilders.

Right: Paul Burke sells a dummy to Crockenhill's Mark Twiner who was within a year to move to Cray.

Right: The Cray defence watch a Crockenhill corner skid across the goalmouth and out for a goal kick.

Right: Cray line up before a Christmas derby fixture against Crockenhill in 1994.
All photos on this page: Mike Floate

Left: A young Jamie Kempster in action for the Wands versus Deal Town in 1994-95. Cray players in the background are Ian Jenkins and goalkeeper David Pike.

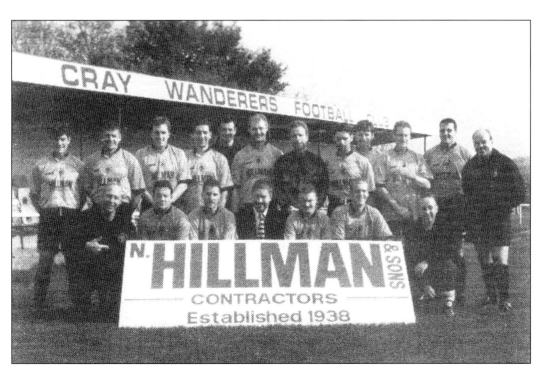

Left: The Hillman era begins. This was the Cray squad in 1995-96.

**Cray Wanderers FC
1860 -2010**

Founded 1860

The quality of football served up by the Wands improved considerably, but a spate of missed penalties and last-minute equalisers meant there was no real progress up the table.
There was a notable achievement by the youth team, who won the London Youth Cup.

The new manager was, though, laying the foundations for a much better team and the addition of Peter Coupland (Herne Bay) and Dave Clark (Slade Green) in particular helped Cray get off to a flying start in 1995-96. In early September, the Wands were actually second in the Kent League, and the side were more than able to hold a mid-table position for the first time in five years.

A League Cup victory at Dartford (now playing at Erith's ground) was particularly pleasant for Ian Jenkins, who beat the Darts' 'keeper Micky Simmons from almost the halfway line. Later, when Simmons joined the Wands, Jenko constantly reminded him of this goal! This game also marked the return of Phil Collins. He was soon amongst the goals again, notching five in a 6-1 win over Faversham.

Off the field, Gary Hillman was already proving a resourceful chairman. Improvements to the Oxford Road ground, including a new entrance and tea-bar, helped make the Cray faithful more cheerful than at any time since the collapse of the Rectory Lane project.

For personal reasons, Whitehead chose not to continue as manager for the following season. His assistant, the popular long-serving defender Glen Cooper, took over the reins for one year. After a poor start, the side soon struck form and Cooper was Manager of the Month for November 1996, with David Pike starring in goal. Both Coupland and Collins, who had notched 40 goals between them in the previous campaign had left, although Collins was to return later in the season. Cooper replaced them with Tunde Utsaja, a powerful striker of Nigerian origin.

Tunde became the focal point of a very direct style of play. In successive away games, the Wands beat Hythe United (League Cup quarter-final), Folkestone Invicta and Ramsgate. The East Kent press took great exception to Cray's approach and decried their: 'Intimidating, powerhouse tactics, which gave a whole new meaning to 'Wham, bam, put snow on it, man' syndrome.' Utsaja, who scored five goals in these games, was described as 'raw', 'explosive' and 'outrageous.'

He possessed perhaps the most powerful shot of any Cray striker and played the game in an unorthodox manner, as this account from *Cray Chatter* of an incident in the Hythe game, shows: 'A full back took the ball off Tunde out by the left touchline, and started to run upfield with the ball.

Right: Cray's top scorers Phil Collins (left) and Peter Coupland in action during a 4-2 win at Herne Bay in 1995-96.

Tunde vowed to get it back, and the means he decided on started with measuring a leap, rather like a long jumper does. Then, in the manner of a Zulu warrior, Tunde made his leap, and judged it to perfection, landing in front of the opposing player and removing the ball from his feet in one swift movement. With no bodily contact made…it seemed not to occur to the referee or his assistant that this was surely a technical foul at least, and play was allowed to continue.'

Left: Tunde scores at Furness in 1996-97.

After this spell of good form, the Wands embarked on a winless run of 17 games, an injury to Tunde being a big factor. This included an agonising exit in extra-time of the League Cup semi-final second leg against Sheppey. Fourth from bottom was a very disappointing final position in a season that saw a new word invented, as Cray 'Tunderised' their opponents!
John Roseman, who had served as Peter Gaydon's assistant some years earlier, was the new manager for 1997-98. He was given the resources to add players of high calibre including goalkeeper Micky Simmons, the Sheppey trio of top striker Steve Marshall and midfielders Jason

Bragg and Perry Weedon, and Jamie McCarthy (Chatham), another high-class forward, who was top scorer with 19.

In fact, the abundance of striking riches proved impossible to maintain and both Marshall and Tunde Utsaja left early in the season. The new line-up proved to be consistent and earned a top six finish, only the second time the club had achieved this since 1985. There were some good cup runs, which fizzled out in the New Year. Greenwich Borough proved to be the bogey side, beating Cray in a Kent Senior Trophy quarter-final replay and the Kent League Cup semi-final, winning the first leg 6-0. They went on to win both competitions.

Left: Johnny Roseman's team in action during 1997-98. Top scorer Jamie McCarthy chases after the ball at Corinthian.

Cray Wanderers FC 1860 -2010

Right: Adam Woods challenges ex-Cray striker Matt Norris in a 1-1 draw with VCD Athletic. Cray players looking on are Marc Cook, Ian Jenkins and Jason Bragg. Note one of the club's most loyal supporters on the touchline!

There was an odd incident in the away game with Sheppey, played at Sittingbourne's giant Central Park ground. Play had to be stopped and the huge main stand evacuated due to a small fire in one of the dressing rooms. The *Kentish Times* produced the inevitable headline, 'Cray's Great Balls of Fire!'

As the season wore on, there was anxiety for the future as the Kent League had decided to form a Premier Division, insisting on floodlights for member clubs. There were problems in organising lights at Oxford Road, and it was only in April that Gary Hillman announced that Cray would ground-share at Bromley F.C. for 1998-99. The Wands bade farewell to Sidcup in style, winning nine of their last ten league games there, including a 2-0 victory against Southern League bound Folkestone.

The visiting press were roundly critical of the playing surface and christened Oxford Road, 'the graveyard of dreams.' Certainly, the ground behind the 'Cons Club' was never one to get too enthusiastic about. Its faults were easy to see: cramped, poor access, with a sloping pitch that was once described as: 'boasting as many blades of grass as hairs on Yul Brynner's head.'

Right: Richard Palmer and Perry Weedon

But there was a cosiness about the place, summed up by the remark in Team Talk magazine that the ground was 'like a well-darned sock.'

And so the Wanderers moved on again, to the Hayes Lane ground, scene of some great triumphs over the years, with a degree of uncertainty as to what the future would hold.

Right: A last look around Oxford Road as the players leave the field after Cray's 4-0 win against Canterbury City at the close of the 1997-98 season.

Jenko takes over

John Roseman decided not to make the move to Hayes Lane, citing a reduced playing budget as his reason for stepping down. This enabled Gary Hillman to make a very significant appointment as Cray's first-team boss; senior player Ian Jenkins was handed the role of player-manager. Surely neither Gary or Jenko could have foreseen the success that their partnership would bring over the next dozen years!

Initially, Jenkins was able to retain most of the previous season's players and he re-captured Tunde Utsaja. Also breaking into the first-team at this time was Jamie Wood, a talented forward player with a sweet left-foot strike. The first game at Hayes Lane was celebrated with a 2-1 victory over VCD Athletic; Billy McCarthy scored the first goal, in front of an encouraging crowd of 127.

The Wands started the 1998-1999 season with a great burst of goalscoring. Tunde was in devastating form, scoring eight in three games. Over a ten-day period, Cray demolished Chatham 6-1 (a fairly even game on the run of play!), squandered a 4-2 lead to lose 5-4 at Tunbridge Wells and then won 5-2 at Whitstable. A month later the return game with Tunbridge Wells also ended 5-4, this time in Cray's favour, with Jenkins helping himself to a hat-trick.

Then, all of a sudden, the goals dried up. From the beginning of December to the end of April, the Wands found the net just 14 times (fewer than they had previously scored in just four games). Nineteen matches passed without a win and several of the best players, including Tunde, drifted away. In five successive home games at Hayes Lane, the Wands failed to score.

At the end of the season, Hillman appointed Fabio Rossi, who had a good track record with Swanley Furness, as manager, believing greater experience was needed at the helm. Ex-player Bob Pittaway came as his assistant; Jenkins was

**Cray Wanderers FC
1860 -2010**

Top: Cray's first home game at Hayes Lane (also their first-ever competitive home game under lights) ended with a 2-1 win against VCD Athletic at the start of the 1998-99 season.

Left: The team in 1999-2000. Back row (L to R): Bobby Pittaway, Jake Watkins, Matt Smith, Marc Petters, Mark Dudley, Mark Brooks, Sean Cooney, Adam Woods, Andre Vincent (Physio). Front row: Peter Cirillo, Jamie Wood, Jon Conran, Adam Heaslewood, Ian Jenkins, Danny Sweeting.

Left: At Cowes (IOW) in 2000-01.

Far left: Mark Brooks collects a cross against Whitstable Town with Adam Woods and John Fellows looking on.

Left: A rainbow at Hayes Lane versus Canterbury City in 2000-01.

Cray Wanderers FC
1860 -2010

Right: Paul McCarthy scores for Cray from the penalty-spot in a 2-1 win at Ramsgate in 2001-02.

retained in a coaching capacity.

Rossi brought with him a host of new players, who had limited senior experience, and they struggled to adapt to Kent League football. A replay victory at Portfield on Cray's return to the F.A. Cup was the only bright spot in a dreadful start to the season. In early October, Ramsgate inflicted a disastrous 7-1 home defeat (Cray's worst for 50 years) and Rossi stepped down. Jenkins and Pittaway took over as joint-managers and conjured up a couple of cup wins, followed by eight successive defeats. As 1999 drew to a close, the Wands were in dire straits. Rock bottom of the Kent League with just four points from 16 games, they had won just three league matches in 14 months!

Gradually, though, the management team began to turn Cray's fortunes around. Some important signings were made, including Mark Loveday, the first of several experienced players to join from landlords Bromley, reliable defender Adam Woods and the fearsome Pietro Cirillo, who stiffened up the midfield considerably. And two of the players Rossi brought to the club established themselves as key players: Adam Heaslewood

was an intelligent presence in the middle of the park, whilst Danny Sweeting formed a lively forward partnership with Jamie Wood and finished the season as top scorer and the supporters' "Player of the Year."

Perhaps most significantly of all, Tunde returned for a cameo of just a handful of games. He scored in four matches in a row in February, all of which were won. The final game of the month was an exciting 4-3 victory over Chatham, when Loveday scored a remarkable winning goal. Cray were awarded what appeared to be a routine free-kick on halfway. But, spotting the Chats' goalkeeper slightly off his line, Loveday launched a huge kick that sailed 60 yards into the net. This sealed the Manager of the Month award for Jenkins. In a remarkable contrast to the previous year, Cray climbed the table to finish in a

Right: Mark Hammond and Drew Watkins in the wall as the Wands defend a free-kick at Bracknell Town in 2001-02.

respectable 13th place. Jenkins was back in sole charge for the 2000-2001 season, which started well. Had Cray won at Herne Bay in mid-October, they would have gone to the top of the table, but they lost 3-0. There followed another inexplicable

Left: Celebrations after a 4-0 home win against Beckenham Town at the end of the 2000-01 season.

slump in form (two wins in twenty) with goalscoring again a problem. Sweeting left for Beckenham in January, but remained leading scorer at the end of the season with just eight goals. In a repeat of events twenty years earlier, Cray even managed to have four players sent off in the closing stages of a game at Erith Town.

Another finish in the wrong half of the table was a disappointment, but some important signings were made, and they played an important role in the success that followed. Ex-Bromley manager, Frank Coles, brought his experience as a player, Joe Vines and Mark Willy would develop into accomplished defenders and Lewis Wood gave the first indications of his goal poaching instincts.

Going for promotion

Now well established at Hayes Lane, Gary Hillman decided it was time for Cray Wanderers to make a serious challenge for honours. The summer of 2001 was a very significant turning point for the club. After twenty years of generally mediocre performances in the Kent League and no

Left: Mark Hammond waits before scoring Cray's 1-0 winner at Sandy Lane versus Tooting in 2001-02.

prospect of advancement, there was a definite strategy that it was time for the club to progress. Now playing at a well-equipped ground, it was even possible to think in terms of promotion to a higher league.

Jenkins was provided with the resources to begin to assemble a team that would challenge for honours. Micky Simmons returned to command the penalty area, Chris Tuley from Thamesmead was an effective striker who finished top scorer with 14, whilst the mercurial Mark Hammond, a highly skilful player and excellent with a dead ball, had his best season for the Wands. Rather confusingly, two players called Paul McCarthy were signed, but the most important capture of

Left: Frank Coles Testimonial: Bromley versus Cray (with several guest players) in 2001-02.

Cray Wanderers FC 1860 -2010

Right: Lewis Wood was a prolific scorer for Cray's reserve team before receiving his first team call-up. Cray continued to play reserve games at Oxford Road after the first team's move to Hayes Lane in 1998.

all proved to be Joe Francis, who had played at the highest levels of non-league football. He played throughout the 2001-02 season, but his biggest contribution has been as Jenko's assistant. A perceptive and highly-imaginative coach, he formed a perfect partnership with the manager, which has been the bedrock of the Wands' success in recent years.

The strengthened side soon made an impact. They won eleven home games in succession in the autumn and moved into second place in the table. An application for promotion to the Southern League was made. Good progress was made in cup competitions. Isthmian sides Hornchurch, Barking and Tooting were all defeated in the London Senior Cup. The victory over Tooting, in their final season at the vast Sandy Lane ground, was one of seven successive away wins, the best run for 20 years.

Sadly, though, after a great 3-1 victory over fellow title challengers Deal Town in the Kent Senior Trophy semi-final, the side's form fell away in the last two months of the season, with only one win in 11 games. Cray failed to

EYES DOWN: Steve Lovell in the thick of the action Ref:Pd294049

BALL WATCHING: Lords on the chase during their Go Travel Kent League defeat against Cray on Saturday Ref:Pd296066

Right: Cray (in blue) win 3-1 at Lordswood in 2002-03. Top: Phil Turner tackles Steve Lovell. Below: Mark Dudley in action.

overcome Whitstable in a two-legged semi-final in the Kent League Cup and succumbed rather meekly to Thamesmead in the Kent Senior Trophy final.

The final league position of 5th was below expectations, but there was some excitement in the last home game of the season. Needing a win to clinch the league title ahead of Maidstone, VCD led Cray 2-1 deep into injury time. Then, in a rare playing appearance, Ian Jenkins bundled the ball home from a corner, to the huge excitement of the Stones' contingent at Hayes Lane, who engulfed him in celebration. It was later suggested on a messageboard that a statue of Jenko should be erected in Maidstone town centre!

Cray Reserves, who continued to play at Oxford Road, had an excellent season under Sam Wright's management. They were denied the league title as a result of a points deduction, incurred through unwittingly naming an ineligible substitute for one game (and he didn't even make it onto the pitch!).

Having denied VCD the league title, Jenkins proceeded to rub salt into the wounds by signing up three of their best players for the 2002-03 season. Ricky Bennett had an excellent scoring record at Kent League level and duly proceeded to score 47 in two seasons for Cray. Richard Dimmock was a powerful presence, with excellent touch for a big man, whilst Phil Turner was highly effective in midfield and was made club captain.

A further trio of signings from Bromley made the Wands into a formidable squad. Ian Rawlings had played over 500 times for the Lilywhites at the heart of their defence, many alongside centre-back partner, David Gray, who also had an eye for goal. Full-back Andy Silk slotted in at full-back and was a great encourager of the team.

The new-look side immediately impressed. At Isthmian League Oxford City in the F.A. Cup, the

Cray Wanderers
Kent League Champions

Photo: Mark Avenell
www.Avenellphotos.com

quality of their passing football was, at times, breathtaking, as they completely outclassed their higher-ranked opponents. A Drew Watkins thunderbolt sealed the win and their was further prize money from the F.A., after Mark Tompkins (another ex-Bromley man) scored the only goal in the next round at Hayes Lane, as Whyteleafe became another Isthmian scalp.

However, the cup run ended at Hemel Hempstead and was followed by a very poor run of form, culminating in a home defeat to lowly Greenwich Borough, which left Cray 15 points behind leaders Maidstone. In his programme notes for the next match against Faversham, long-serving editor Greg Mann issued a wake-up call,

"For a team supposedly aiming for one of the top spots this year we were downright awful. A complete lack of commitment was evident and I'm sorry to say that if that attitude continues the players could well be playing in front of an empty ground 'cause sure as hell nobody is going to pay to watch it."

Perhaps this did the trick, as in front of just 59 spectators, Cray won 8-0! Performances improved: Bennett got four-goal hauls against Erith and Whitstable and Dimmock notched a ten-minute hat-trick against Herne Bay in the Kent Senior Trophy.

Although a 2-1 win over Maidstone (attendance 321) was welcome, there still seemed far too much ground to make up, especially when a run of fourteen matches unbeaten came to an end at home to Thamesmead (1-2), with Bennett suffering a season-ending injury. Jamie Wood returned to replace him and scored a hat-trick against Tunbridge Wells to secure the Wands a place in the Kent League Cup final for the first time in nineteen games.

Five star Cray

CRAY Wanderers made it 16 goals from their last three matches with a comprehensive 5-0 demolition of Erith Town at Hayes Lane last Wednesday.

The main surprise was the fact that it took until the 38th minute for the deadlock to be broken when Ricky Bennett found the target from close range.

The same player doubled the advantage just after the hour mark as he converted Mark Hammond's free-kick with an audacious back heel from six yards out.

Bennett's hat-trick was completed in the 78th minute with a fine opportunist effort as the home side stepped up a gear.

Within 90 seconds the lead was extended even further as Andy Silk got his name on the scoresheet for the second week running.

The rout was complete seven minutes from time as Bennett claimed his fourth, converting from the edge of the box.

CRAY: Simmons, Silk (Jenkins), Rawlings, Gray (Coles), Taylor, Dudley, Cooney (Cirillo), Wakins, Turner, Bennett, Hammond, Sub: Francis.
ERITH: Arnold, Hanlon, McAlpine, Reeves, Coburn, Edwards (Wright), Holt, Smith, Pressney, Jukes (Putnam), Hackett, Subs: Terry, Clark.

Cray Wanderers FC
1860 -2010

Founded 1860

Far left: 'Championi!'

Left: Closing in on the Kent League championship in 2002-03.

per Wands march on

CRAY WANDERERS FC

TH ME: Cray Wanderers fly the flag for the Kent League before their trip north last Friday.   contribute

ent Celtic 0
erers 1

Wanderers
the last 16
se after a 1-
over West
Celtic last

rike by Jamie
the difference
es as a backs to
saw the Kent
pions safely

l by the late with-
ve pillar David
led out due to a

ned brightly and
contest wrapped

th minute strike
enough to warm
ong a healthy

ll down 35 yards
left goalkeeper
the spot as his
into the top cor-

had more to show
macy as Ricky
mpster and Wood
ecently.
ed a good early
re Wood crossed
uld not force the

One superb move saw Bennett hit a delightful ball down the line to Kempster but his first time centre was flashed wide by Wood.

Celtic had an opening of their own but goalkeeper Micky Simmons denied Alex Benjamin with his left knee.

In a role reversal, the Cray defenders took centre stage in the second half.

But it could have been different if Kempster had not wasted a golden opportunity two minutes after the break.

As it was, Danny Whelan and Ian Rawlings had to perform heroics and Simmons turned in a faultless display.

Chances

The home side created chance after chance. Benjamin had a header cleared off the line by Rawlings. Dave Malone had a free-kick brilliantly tipped over the crossbar, while Andy Bowman and Benjamin were thwarted in quick succession.

But the real drama came right at the death when Rawlings thought he had sealed the victory on 82 minutes. His shot beat the goalkeeper but Malone scrambled back to clear the ball off the line.

Rawlings then limped out of the game after denying Bowman before Simmons defied the years to make a world class save to deny Bowman.

CRAY: Simmons, Silk, Whelan, Rawlings, Evans, Hesslewood (Myall 53), Turner, Kempster, P Dimmock (S Wood 67), Bennett (Taylor 84), J Wood. Subs: R Dimmock

Professionalism pleases Cray chief

CHAIRMAN Gary Hillman has praised the professional approach of manager Ian Jenkins and assistant Joe Francis after their FA Vase victory last Saturday, *writes Matthew Panting.*

The Wands reached the last 16 with a hard-fought win at Newcastle-based West Allotment Celtic.

It meant an overnight stay, a long flight north and a morning training session for the Cray squad, but Hillman said that they came through with flying colours.

"It was a really good weekend and the result obviously went for us," said Hillman.

"The boys were exceptional and the way they went about the job was excellent.

"Full credit to Ian and Joe, they made sure it was a professional outfit.

"I don't think the media and the staff up there could believe how professional we were in the hotel and how focused we were before the game.

"In the end, it was a case of holding on for the win

but we put a lot of effort into it and deserved to go through."

None have put more into Cray this season than Hillman, who has steered the club to the brink of glory.

Still chasing honours in cup competitions, they are on course to claim the league championship for the second successive season and have confirmed their aspiration to move up the football pyramid this time.

"We're still in the London Cup and Kent Cup but the League and the FA Vase are obviously our main priorities," added Hillman.

"We've applied for promotion and the league above us next season could be something special if the restructuring all goes through.

"It could be really good and it would make sense for any club in the Kent League to try and get involved.

"There will probably be derby matches nearly every week and the support will be excellent in that divi-

sion. If we got promoted it would really push Cray on as a club in non-league circles as well."

Promotion issues will be considered at the end of the season but of more immediate focus for Cray will be their fifth round FA Vase game, away to Screwfix Direct Western League outfit Keynsham Town.

The Somerset side are languishing in 13th place but caused an upset in the previous round by knocking out United Counties outfit St Neots Town, who had previously disposed of Kent League Thamesmead.

"We wanted a home draw but we have to be pleased with what came out of the hat," said Hillman.

"Ian and Joe are too professional to take any game lightly and we will do our homework and prepare in the right fashion."

Cray will be looking to reach the last eight of the competition for the second time in their history.

They previously made the quarter-final stage in 1979/80 before losing to eventual winners Stamford.

Cray Wanderers FC 1860 -2010

Right: *Cray pressure on the Keynsham goal in the F.A. Vase 5th round … but it needed extra time before Matt Woolf broke the deadlock. Jamie Wood later added a second for the Wands.*

Maidstone began to stutter, but still looked a good side when they beat Cray 3-0 in the Kent Senior Trophy final at Chatham on Easter Saturday. No-one amongst the Wands supporters who trooped home disappointed could have anticipated the drama that was to unfold over the following ten days.

• Easter Monday: Maidstone drop two more League points. Remarkably, Cray can now overhaul them.
• Tuesday: Cray beat Ramsgate 4-2 at Hayes Lane, thanks to another Wood hat-trick.
• Friday: the Kent League Committee decide what to do about bottom club Faversham who have folded with eight fixtures unplayed. Everyone assumes either their record will be expunged or their opponents will be awarded wins, but the Committee apply the little-known Rule 14 (b), which states that the title will be decided on "points per game average." The arithmetic of this is that the title is out of Cray's

hands again. Once the implications sink in, there is outrage amongst the Wands supporters.
• Saturday: Maidstone need only to beat Ramsgate to clinch the title. If they slip up, a win for Thamesmead will give them the crown. Cray's game with Slade Green seems academic. But, in an afternoon of high drama, Maidstone and Thamesmead both draw, whilst Cray win 2-0.
• Tuesday: Cray need to beat Lordswood at Hayes Lane to win the Kent League for the first time in 22 years. After 77 agonising minutes, with the score still goalless, David Gray slams the ball home and Richard Dimmock adds a second.

The celebrations lasted long into the night, but the team recovered sufficiently to clinch the double, beating VCD in the League Cup final a few days later. And the Reserves made it a "double double" by winning Division One (North) and the Reserve League Cup. The goalscoring of Lewis Wood and Paul Vines was the key to their success.

No application had been made for promotion and a warning note was sounded by Gary Hillman in the close-season, as he suggested that the club needed new blood to take it forward and that he would step down after one more year. Two top players did leave for higher-ranked clubs (Willy to Bromley and Watkins to Folkestone) but Jenkins made the important signing of Maidstone's midfield dynamo Jamie Kempster and also persuaded Micky Simmons to delay the retirement he had previously announced.

Right: *David Gray and Ian Rawlings defend the Cray goal during the 1-0 win against Hythe Town in the Kent Senior Trophy final at Ashford in 2003-04.*

SANDWICHED: Hythe's Scott Porter (centre) is squeezed out by Cray during the Kent Senior Trophy final   Ref: pd 57321P

Cray chase the treble

Building on their success, the side started the 2003-04 season in blistering form. The rock-solid defence went a record six games without conceding a goal, progress was made through the first three rounds of the F.A. Cup for the first time ever and Sporting Bengal United were welcomed into the Kent League with a 10-0 thumping at Hayes Lane.

Goals were flying in from all over the park. In midfield, Kempster opened his scoring account with a hat-trick against Pagham in the F.A. Cup and had netted 22 at the turn of the year, whilst Adam Heaslewood notched 11 by the end of November. David Gray continued to stroll forward to find the net with regularity, new signing Matt Woolf chipped in usefully and Richard Dimmock scored four as bogey side Thamesmead were hammered 6-0 away from home in the Kent Senior Trophy.

Cray didn't lose a league game until December and opened up a commanding lead at the top of the table, with only VCD able to cling on to their coat tails. Good progress was made in all the cup competitions, but it was the F.A. Vase that captured the most interest.

An exciting third-round encounter with Great Yarmouth was settled by an extra-time free-kick by Ross Lover. Lover, a clever midfield player with great composure and awareness on the ball, was one of two young "gems" who came through from the reserve team. The other was Sam Wood, an excellent left-sided player, who, after a spell at Bromley, moved on to play League football for Brentford.

In the last 32 of the Vase, Cray were faced with their longest-ever away trip, to north of Newcastle to play West Allotment Celtic, leaders of the Northern Alliance. The journey was made by air and drew a record attendance to the host's very soggy ground near Whitley Bay. It was a difficult afternoon for the Wands, but they won through thanks to a fantastic strike by Jamie Wood, followed by his trademark gymnastic celebration. Ian Rawlings and Danny Whelan played superbly at the back to preserve the lead.

The next round brought another trip, this time to the West Country where Cray saw off the challenge of Keynsham Town. Missed chances meant extra-time was necessary, before the two vital goals were scored. The Wands had equalled their best performance by reaching the quarter-finals.

Although there was no prospect of going to Wembley, due to the stadium's redevelopment, a place in the Vase final was very much in their sights.

A.F.C. Sudbury were the visitors to Hayes Lane on a day that had many similarities to Cray's previous F.A. Vase quarter-final 24 years earlier. There was a record crowd (771) for a Wands game at the ground, the opponents were strong

Left: Cray's F.A. Vase run came to an end in the quarter-final at home to A.F.C. Sudbury in 2003-04.

Cray Wanderers FC
1860 -2010

and uncompromising, the game went into extra-time goalless, there was a repeat of the crowd misbehaviour that had occurred at Oxford Road... and Cray bowed out in the additional period.

Cray had to ride out a 'post-Vase slump' which included last-gasp league defeats to Whitstable (after leading 2-0) and Thamesmead. This enabled VCD to close the gap at the top. Cray gained some psychological advantage when they beat Vickers on penalties in the Kent Senior Trophy semi-final, but a late equaliser by Jon Main for VCD in the league game at Hayes Lane kept the title race very tight.

But it was Cray who kept their nerve to cross the finishing line. Rawlings powered home a last-minute header to clinch the Kent Senior Trophy after a very tight final against in-form Hythe at Ashford. It was the Wands' second victory in the competition, after the disappointment of two defeats in a row in the final.

A week later, Cray fell behind in the vital league game at VCD, but a superb second-half performance turned things round completely. The 3-1 victory brought the title within reach, and it was duly secured two days later with a win over Hythe at Hayes Lane.

The Reserves again added to a very successful season for the club by retaining the League Cup and winning the Kent Intermediate Cup for the first time in nearly 40 years, on penalties against Whitstable. But, as the season came towards it close, thoughts turned to the tantalising prospect of promotion, something Cray Wanderers had been seeking, on and off, for nearly 50 years.

Rumours and counter-rumours were heard before, during and after the Kent League Cup final against Thamesmead, which a depleted Cray side lost 1-0. At one stage, it looked bleak for Cray; apparently clubs that groundshared might not be promoted. But, thanks to the behind-the-scenes advocacy of Gary Hillman and Cray's friends in the Kent League hierarchy, the announcement was made the Wands would have a place in the Ryman Isthmian League Division One for the 2004-05 season.

There is no doubt that this was an absolutely critical decision for the future of the club. If promotion had not been achieved, it is likely that the team would have broken up, Gary Hillman might have carried out his intention to step down, and the progress made at Hayes Lane would have been wasted. Having won ten league championships since 1957, few could argue that promotion was not deserved.

Cray had finally made it to the Isthmian League! One would like to think that former-chairman Mick Slater, God rest his soul, was celebrating too.

Right: Promoted! After winning the Kent League championship again in 2003-04 the Wands secured promotion into the Ryman League. Back row (L to R): John de Palma (Physio), Paul Foley, Robert Browning, Danny Evans, John Mayall, Micky Simmons, David Gray, James Taylor, Richard Dimmock, Danny Whelan, Ian Rawlings, John Allwright. Front row: Andy Silk, Jamie Wood, Sam Wood, Adam Heaslewood, Joe Francis (Assistant Manager), Gary Hillman (Chairman), Ian Jenkins (Manager), Jamie Kempster, Ross Lover, Matt Woolf, Ricky Bennett.

Getting established in the Ryman League

Cray supporters may have had to pinch themselves when they saw the fixture list for the club's first season at the higher level. The Wands now found themselves competing on equal terms as such famous non-league names as Walton & Hersham, Tooting & Mitcham, Dulwich Hamlet, Leatherhead and their land-lords, Bromley. With the majority of their successful side remaining, Jenkins and Francis reinforced the squad with two top Kent League strikers: Michael Power (Thamesmead) and Leigh Bremner (Herne Bay). Also signing was defender Danny Bower, who had League experience with Fulham, and the adaptable Dean Morris.

The Wands warmed up for their Ryman adventure by beating Thamesmead in the Kent League Charity Shield game, a week before the historic day of their first Isthmian League game, a trip to Sussex to play Burgess Hill Town. Cray dominated proceedings but fell a goal behind, only for late strikes from Kempster and Bremner to ensure a memorable outcome for the Wanderers.

In fact, Cray made a splendid start in their new surroundings. It was nine games before they lost and a remarkable 11 goals were scored in two away matches, at Corinthian Casuals and New-

Cray Wanderers FC
1860 -2010

Left: Cray (in blue) find the net in their 6-0 win at Newport (IOW) in 2004-05.

port (Isle of Wight), Bremner notching six. After a slight stutter that brought no wins in five games, the squad was strengthened further as Drew Watkins and Phil Collins returned to the club. Collins, who had always promised to end his career at Cray, had enjoyed a sparkling period of goalscoring since leaving the Wands, rising to the Conference National with Margate.

Phil's return led to comments about Cray's links with the music industry, as he joined David Gray and midfielder James Taylor in the side. Sadly, John Mayall, who had been a useful squad member, had recently left the club!

Collins was on target immediately as Cray won their first-ever F.A. Trophy game (3-1 v Aveley), but it was Bremner who hit the headlines when the Wands took on Bromley in a league match for the first time in 90 years. His superb hat-trick was the centrepiece of a wonderful 5-2 win for Cray that ensured local bragging rights, at least for a while.

There were so many highlights in what was an incredibly enjoyable time for Cray's supporters: Jamie Wood's two left-foot strikes that flew in "like arrows" at Hastings, further progress in the Trophy, beating Folkestone after extra-time before narrowly losing in a replay at St Albans and a thrilling 4-3 win at Walton & Hersham who were on a run of 13 straight wins.

Left: Jamie Kempster fires home in the return fixture that Cray won 5-0. Photo: Trevor Mulligan.

Left, bottom: Line-up before the 1-1 draw with Tooting & Mitcham on August Bank Holiday 2004. Back row (L to R): John Mayall, Richard Dimmock, Drew Watkins, David Gray, Tony Russell, Robert Browning, Dean Mann, James Taylor, James Millar. Front row: John de Palma (physio), John Myatt, Dean Morris, Leigh Bremner, Jamie Wood, Sam Wood, Ross Lover.

Cray Wanderers FC 1860 -2010

Right: Danny Bower heads home in Cray's 3-2 win versus Fleet Town in 2004-05.

A Bromley supporter summed up the quality of Cray's football: "I'd like to congratulate Cray on a fantastic display. They showed what it takes to win games in this league: solid defence, speedy attacks, hard work, desire & team spirit."

The icing on the cake, though, was the win against AF.C. Wimbledon. The re-formed side were running away with the league and came to Hayes Lane on a record run of 78 league games unbeaten. In front of a new highest gate of 1,082, James Millar gave Cray an early lead, but it was Sam Wood who brought the house down in the second half as his brilliant solo goal ensured a moment of national fame for the Wands.

Cray kept up with the leading group throughout the season, but too many draws proved costly; after 32 league games, exactly half had been drawn. Power returned to form with ten goals in eight games, as six straight wins secured the Wands a play-off place. But defeats to the top four teams at the end of the season showed that Cray were not yet quite good enough for another promotion. Bromley beat them 3-2 in the return

game. Wimbledon and Walton got their revenge (the gate at Wimbledon was a huge 3,358).

Finally, after leading for a long-time in the play-off semi-final, and holding on thanks to some great saves by 'keeper Steve Northwood, Cray succumbed 3-1 in extra-time at Horsham.

Nevertheless, it had been an outstanding opening campaign for Cray. They were top scorers in the entire Ryman League.

Right: The Cray team that reached the Ryman Division One South play-offs in their first season 2004-05. Back row (L to R): John de Palma (physio), Danny Bower, David Gray, James Taylor, Tony Russell, Phil Collins, Michael Power, Ian Rawlings, Ross Lover, Ian Jenkins, Joe Francis. Front row: Dean Morris, John Myatt, Steve Northwood, Leigh Bremner, Jamie Wood, Jamie Kempster, Matt Woolf, Sam Wood, James Millar, Drew Watkins

Cray Wanderers FC
1860 -2010

Expectations were very high for 2005-06, as Jenkins added non-league goalscoring legend Gary Abbott (a semi-pro international) and the prolific Jon Main to the strikeforce. Cray raced to the top of the table with four wins and embarked on a record-breaking F.A. Cup run. In the Preliminary Round at Steyning Town, with Cray leading 4-0, Jenko brought himself on in the closing stages in an obvious attempt to extend his amazing goalscoring record. He duly nodded home a corner and retired back to the bench, having scored a goal in 14 successive seasons for the Wands.

Left: Jamie Wood

A Michael Power hat-trick accounted for Kingstonian in the next round, in a game that saw six players dismissed, three from each side. Further victories over Camberley and Margate (a convincing 3-0 win over a Ryman Premier side) took Cray to the final qualifying round for the first time in their history. Unfortunately, standing between them and a game with a Football

Left: Ross Lover.

Cray Wanderers FC 1860 -2010

Right: F.A. Cup fever in 2005-06 as Cray beat Margate to reach the 4th qualifying round for the first time ever in their history.

Far right: Joe Francis hailed this as the best football ever played by a Cray side up to that time, mid-season 2005-06.

Right: Jenko holds the F.A. Cup ... but the Wands were beaten 2-0 by Conference leaders Grays Athletic after a brave display.

RED, AMBER, GO

Cray stun Margate to set up Grays clash

full match report on p70

League club, were Grays Athletic, leaders of the Conference National. The Wands played with great determination and were not disgraced in losing 2-0, in a game in which Northwood was outstanding.

Almost unnoticed during the cup run, six league games had been lost. It was such inconsistency, often the result of a build-up of injuries, which cost Cray any prospect of mounting a promotion challenge. There were some highlights, especially at home. Main's hat-trick against Premier

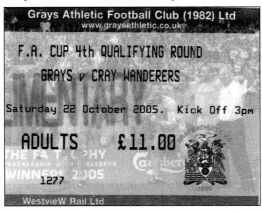

Grays Athletic Football Club (1982) Ltd
www.graysathletic.co.uk

F.A. CUP 4th QUALIFYING ROUND

GRAYS v CRAY WANDERERS

Saturday, 22 October 2005. Kick Off 3pm

ADULTS £11.00

1277
WestvieW Rail Ltd

HANDS OFF: Mark Stimson, right, grapples with Ian Jenkins for the FA Cup
PICTURE: Martin Dalton

Division Staines in the F.A. Trophy (Cray won 4-3) gave a glimpse of his potential; he scored 20 goals before leaving for Tonbridge early in the New Year. Bremner scored a brilliant hat-trick against Leatherhead to haul Cray back from 3-0 down for a 3-3 draw. And, towards the end of the season, the Wands showed what they might have achieved as Horsham and Tonbridge (who were both promoted) and Dover were defeated at Hayes Lane.

Main is electric as Wanderers power through

A SUPERB second-half hat-trick by Jon Main was the highlight as Cray once again showed their appetite for cup football this season, *writes Jerry Dowlen.*

The Wands were not expected to beat their third-placed Ryman Premier opponents, but got off to a flyer with just 35 seconds on the clock.

Drew Watkins drove in a free-kick, Gary Abbott nodded the ball into the goalmouth at the far post and Michael Power headed home.

The visitors quickly asserted themselves and attacked powerfully, but Craig Maskell's eighth minute equaliser was a lucky rebound off Cray defender David Hall's attempted clearance after Jermaine Hunter's deflected shot hit the post.

Power brought two saves from Shaun Allaway but Staines were looking to bully Cray out of the game and ominously took the lead on 44 minutes when Hunter headed home.

Under-pressure Cray conceded a free-kick on the edge of the box a minute later, but Steve Northwood dived at full stretch to block the shot and bravely grab the loose ball after it rolled invitingly to Hunter's feet.

That proved to be a crucial save as Cray raised their game in the second half.

Watkins and Power skilfully put Main through to finish coolly on 50 and 55 minutes after out-running the Staines

Cray Wanderers	4
(Power 1, Main 50, 55, 85)	
Staines Town	**3**
(Maskell 8, Hunter 44, de Lisser 56)	

FA TROPHY

defence.

Andre de Lisser cracked home an equaliser for Staines a minute later, but the longer the game went on, it was Cray - playing accurate passing football - who looked more likely to win it.

Terry Khan and Ian Rawlings were outstanding in defence to keep the visitors at bay, and the game moved into its dramatic climax in the last 12 minutes.

Main fluffed a penalty-kick on 78 minutes, shooting weakly at Allaway who had brought him down inside the box after Cray speared through the Staines defence again.

But Main had the perfect answer when a flowing move upfield saw Power cleverly work the ball through to him five minutes from time.

The young Cray striker produced an outstanding finish with a curling shot high into the far corner of the net to secure a thrilling victory for the Wands.

Cray Wanderers: Northwood, Hall, Rawlings, Morris, Khan, Taylor (Lover 46), Power (Ward 89), Kempster, Abbott (Bremner 60), Main, Watkins. Subs not used: Baker, Wood.

Although they again started strongly with three wins, the 2006-07 season was Cray's least successful in the Ryman League Division One. Ian Rawlings and David Gray decided to hang up their boots; both had made a wonderful contribution to the club's success over a four-year period. Their replacements were Al-James Hannigan, with his vast experience at the top of the non-league game, and Mark Willy, who was warmly welcomed on his return from Bromley. Another popular signing was classy left-back Colin Luckett from Bromley, who had had a long and successful spell with Kingstonian, including appearing in the F.A. Trophy final at Wembley.

Cray showed glimpses of their potential in a commanding performance when they beat Dartford 4-0 at Hayes Lane. There was a good F.A. Trophy run in which Luckett netted with superb free-kicks against Cheshunt and Yeading and Lover scored a "wonder goal" at Waltham Forest, showing immense skill to volley home a cross that seemed to come straight down from the sky.

Lewis Wood marked his return to the club by

heading the scoring charts with 15 but it was his brother Jamie who reached a big landmark when he scored his 100th goal for the club at Tooting. A consistent player who made an important contribution every season at Hayes Lane, he was once described as having "probably the best left foot in the league." This report was typical of his goals,

"The impressive Jamie Wood, who was a constant thorn in Town's side…ran at Town's defence before unleashing an unstoppable left-foot shot from the edge of the penalty area."

Cray's only chance of silverware in 2007 came in the Ryman League Cup. Abbott put on a masterclass in finishing at Premier Division Boreham Wood in the quarter-final, scoring both in a 2-1 win, but he was injured soon after and did not play again. In fact, a spate of injuries and departures (the popular Bremner and Northwood both moved on) unsettled the side. Experienced ex-Football League players Gareth Graham and Andy Martin were amongst those brought in to plug the gaps, but the season fizzled out disappointingly. By the time Cray travelled to Dover in the League Cup semi-final, they had only the barebones of a side of eligible players. Defender Matt Lee suffered a horrendous injury in this game, which Cray lost 4-3. The fact that Ian Jenkins scored for the 15th season running was little or no consolation.

Left: Gary Abbott was an experienced new signing for the Wands in 2005-06.

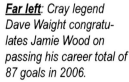

Far left: Cray legend Dave Waight congratulates Jamie Wood on passing his career total of 87 goals in 2006.

Left: Al-James Hannigan was another veteran who added strength to the Wands squad. He is seen here after scoring versus Croydon Athletic in 2006-07.

**Cray Wanderers FC
1860 -2010**

Founded 1860

__Right__: Mark Willy.

A second promotion is achieved

Cray re-grouped at the start of the 2007-08 season, bringing in the experienced Glen Knight as goalkeeper and Danny Chapman (over 70 appearances for Leyton Orient in the Football League) in midfield. Arron Day from Tooting proved to be a dependable right-back, whilst Ryan Royston helped to shore up the defence. The exciting Tyrone Sterling offered real threat on the left wing.

The campaign started indifferently with too many goals being conceded, including six against AF.C. Wimbledon in the F.A. Cup and five in a disastrous home defeat to Ashford. But the signing of defender Steve Aris from Fisher Athletic coincided with the start of a magnificent run of 28 unbeaten league games. At last, the consistency that had been lacking in previous seasons was achieved.

*Colin Luckett (__far right__)
and Michael Power in
action during Cray's
record-breaking run of
28 games without defeat
in the Ryman League in
2007-08.*

**Cray Wanderers FC
1860 -2010**

*Action during a 2-1 win
against Dulwich Hamlet*

Photos: Dave West

Cray Wanderers FC
1860 -2010

Founded 1860

Power had his best season for the club as the focal point of the attack, Lover, with increasing maturity, dominated the midfield and the defence conceded well under a goal a game.

The biggest highlight of this period actually came in the Kent Senior Cup. Cray were drawn "at home" to Bromley in the semi-final. The large crowd at Hayes Lane was stunned as the Wands completely overpowered Bromley's full-strength Conference South side 6-1 to put themselves in the final for the first time in over a hundred years.

Unfortunately, Dover had built up an unassailable lead at the top of the table and, with only one side promoted automatically, Third-placed Cray would have to rely on the play-offs if they were to achieve promotion.

Right: Tyrone Sterling

Standing in their way were the formidable Tooting & Mitcham, who had already met Cray four times and had won three. After the Wands had seen off Met. Police 2-0 in a semi-final delayed by a waterlogged pitch, Cray travelled to meet second-placed Tooting in the play-off final.

With under 48 hours to prepare and with Power and 15-goal strike partner George Fenwick both far from fit, the odds were stacked against Cray in the "winner takes all" game, played in front of 939 at Imperial Fields. In an even game of few chances, the winner came near the end, scored

for Tooting by former Cray player Paul Vines. It was a heartbreaking way to end an excellent season. Cray were named Ryman Division One South "team of the season" and, significantly, they won the Fair Play Award. But the biggest prize had eluded them.

Right: The Cray team that finished third in Ryman Division One South in 2007-08.
Back row (L to R): Joe Francis, Ross Lover, Ryan Royston, Tommy Whitnell, Glen Knight, Tyrone Sterling, Michael Power, Mark Willy, Arron Day, Danny Chapman. Front row: Jamie Kempster, Dean Morris, Jamie Wood, Lewis Wood, David Hall, Colin Luckett, Steve Aris, Ian Jenkins.

Cray Wanderers FC
1860 -2010

Left: *Ian Jenkins joins Gary Hillman (Chairman) and John Woolf (Vice-Chairman) as they announce the Sandy Lane new ground project for Cray Wanderers FC.*

Middle left: *Ian Jenkins receives the Ryman manager of the month award from Barry Simmons.*

Far left: *Ian Jenkins and Danny Chapman.*

Cray Wanderers 3 Burgess Hill Tn 0

By JERRY DOWLEN

LEWIS WOOD bagged a double as Cray easily saw-off ten man Burgess Hill.

The visitors finished with ten after Nick Fogdon was sent off for handball in the 65th minute.

In the 39th minute Tyrone Sterling's low cross was fired home by the appropriately-named Richmond Kissi for a Cray goal on Valentines Day.

Steve Harper missed a chance to equalise after the break with only Glen Knight to

beat before Ashley Carr also went close for the Hillians.

A crunching tackle by skipper Jamie Kempster set up Cray's second goal on 75 minutes.

The ball was fed to Kissi and he sent it through for Wood, who finished the chance expertly.

And Wood tapped home to make it three with five minutes remaining.

STAR MAN: Jamie Kempster (Cray) MATCH RATING ★★★★☆

There was a real sense that it was "promotion or bust" as the 2008-09 season began. The star signing was Shawn Beveney, an experienced international for Guyana, who had ambitions to play professionally. Tooting's Scott Kinch added a combative element to midfield, alongside the experience of ex-Millwall professional Tony Dolby. On the minus side, there were the losses of Lover, Power, Fenwick and Lewis Wood.

The Kent Senior Cup final from the previous season was finally played in July, Ebbsfleet United comfortably beating a well below-strength

Cray side 4-0. The first-half of the campaign was not particularly encouraging. Although the Wands kept on terms with the leaders in a very open league, they suffered big defeats to all of their main rivals. The best results of the autumn were a 2-1 F.A. Trophy victory at Premier Division Horsham and an 8-1 win at Corinthian Casuals (a Ryman League record for Cray) in which Kinch scored five. Youngster Tom Whitnell made a good contribution in the first-half of the season, with 12 goals and Bremner returned in November. Beveney was released as he failed to recapture form after a lengthy injury break.

By early February, the Wands had already suffered nine league defeats and they looked to be slipping out of the play-off places when they trailed lowly Leatherhead at Hayes Lane. But inspired by Richmond Kissi (promoted from the Reserves) and Lewis Wood, back for yet another spell, Cray turned the game round with a late winner. It proved to be a turning point, as the side embarked on a run of eight successive wins.

Confidence grew as Kent rivals Ashford, Sittingbourne and Folkestone were all defeated away from home. Willy had a magnificent time at the heart of the defence, Chapman was hugely influential as the holding midfield player and the signing of ex-Crystal Palace and Wolves star Simon Osborn added a touch of class to the side. In a league where no other side was able to string a consistent set of results together, at one point Cray headed the league by six points,

Below: *Simon Osborn nets versus Met Police and celebrates his promotion-winning goal (left). Photos: Trevor Mulligan.*

Cray Wanderers FC
1860 -2010

Right: The open-top bus tour of Bexley, the Crays, Orpington and Sidcup in May 2009 to celebrate promotion and to announce the Sandy Lane new ground project.

although Kingstonian had games in hand. A disappointing home defeat to Whyteleafe and a last minute equaliser by Fleet put a brake on progress, setting up what amounted to a championship decider at Kingsmeadow on Easter Monday. Unfortunately, Cray never recovered from conceding two early goals and had to look again to the play-offs to achieve promotion.

As runners-up, the Wands had home advantage in both matches. A tense evening against Worthing was settled by Jamie Wood's excellent strike just before half-time, earning a place in the final against Met. Police, who had beaten Cray twice in the League. A good crowd of 659 ringing Hayes Lane saw few chances to either side in the first 80 minutes. Then, Osborn stepped up to take a free-kick just outside the box. He found the top corner in expert fashion and triggered huge celebrations amongst Cray's fans, which were repeated on the final whistle and again a few weeks later as the team and supporters took to the streets on an open-top bus parade.

No-one could deny that Cray deserved their second promotion in five years. Great credit is

due to Ian Jenkins, Joe Francis and their assistant Paul Blade along, of course, with Gary Hillman, without whom none of the success that the Wands have enjoyed since the turn of the century would have been possible.

Right: Mark Willy heads home for Cray in a 2-0 win at Ashford Town (Kent).

**Cray Wanderers FC
1860 -2010**

Above: Jack Smelt.

<u>**Far left, top**</u>: *Cray attack the Canvey goal, 2009/10.*

Above: Mark Willy.

<u>**Left**</u>: *Ian and Wendy Jenkins in October 2009 – a presentation to mark Ian's tenth year as manager of the Wands.*

Above: George Porter.

<u>**Below:**</u> *Team line-up before the 3-2 win versus Margate in November 2009. Back row (L to R): John Woolf, Joe Francis, Jerome Maledon, Delano Sam-Yorke, Mark Willy, George Porter, John Guest, Jack Smelt, Arron Day, Tommy Tyne, Rob Quinn, Tyrone Sterling, Steve Aris, Mike Reeves. Front row: Zak Goldsmith, Shane Graham, Leigh Bremner, Jamie Wood, Lewis Wood, Colin Luckett, Ian Jenkins, Paul Blade.*

Cray Wanderers FC
1860 -2010

Right: A last-minute winning goal versus Margate.

Right: 'Ballet in the Rain' versus Margate!

Below: Colin Luckett scores from the penalty-spot versus Dartford in January 2010.

During the close season, the club announced the establishment of a football Academy at Coopers Technology College. Managed by Darren Anslow, building on the important contribution of Mark Hanscombe whose reserve team had been consistently high standard, the project was an instant success, and within twelve months was producing players ready for Ryman Premier Division football. The Academy represented the fulfilment of the mission started by Sam Wright, when he managed Cray's reserve team, of finding and nurturing young players who would eventually take the step up to Jenko's first team.

Efforts were made in the summer to strengthen the playing squad as the Wands prepared for their new adventure of Ryman Premier football in 2009-10. The former Republic of Ireland B International Rob Quinn, who had a long career in the Football League, was drafted in to replace Danny Chapman, who had retired. Tommy Tyne, ex-Tonbridge and Dover, was another important signing.

There was a big turnout of Cray supporters for the historic first-ever Ryman Premier League game just across the river at Aveley, at the start of season 2009-10. Colin Luckett netted from the penalty-spot to register the Wands' landmark first Ryman Premier goal, in a solid 1-1 draw.

However, two home defeats followed and, in echo of previous periods in the club's history when the team had taken a step up to a higher level, it soon became clear the season would be one where Cray team would have to battle hard to hold their own.

**Cray Wanderers FC
1860 -2010**

Founded 1860

Below: *George Porter is fouled to earn a last-minute penalty kick in their final game of the 2009-10 season.
Photo: Trevor Mulligan.*
Bottom: *Simon Osborn scores to earn Cray a 1-1 draw versus Horsham.
It was the second year running that the veteran Osborn had netted Cray's final goal of the season.*

**Cray Wanderers FC
1860 -2010**

Cray's first-ever win in the Ryman Premier came at Tooting & Mitcham, with the long-serving Wood brothers Jamie and Lewis netting the goals in a 2-0 win. There were good away wins at Margate and Hornchurch. However, approaching the end of November, no home wins had been recorded, and the Wands were deep in the relegation dogfight.

Victories over Maidstone and Margate at Hayes Lane boosted morale. In the latter game, George Porter from the Academy scored twice. A lad with tremendous pace, he proved to be an exciting new addition to the strike force. However, no consistency could be found and a dreadful 5-1 defeat at Canvey Island early in the New Year left Cray facing an uphill struggle to prevent their spell in the Ryman Premier League becoming just a "one season wonder."

Ian Jenkins and his management team 'kept the faith' and made some inspired changes. Ross Lover was given a new role at right-back alongside the increasingly solid centre-back pairing of Mark Willy and John Guest, who had arrived from Dartford. A tighter, high-tempo style proved really successful as five of the next six games were won, including excellent victories over promotion-chasing Kingstonian and Boreham Wood.

The tireless Leigh Bremner was top scorer, closely followed by Luckett, whose tally included 10 penalties, many of which were won by Bremner. The judicious use of loan players, including youngsters from Charlton Athletic, was a feature of the second half of the season as Cray maintained their status with two games to spare, finishing in a creditable 15th position.

It was an important achievement to consolidate the club's position at the higher level. Great credit is due to Ian Jenkins, Joe Francis and their assistant Paul Blade along, of course, with Gary Hillman, without whom none of the success that the Wands have enjoyed since the turn of the century would have been possible.

The 150th anniversary of the club's foundation was marked in May and June by an exhibition at Bromley Museum and a Charity Ball in aid of the 'Bromley Y' charity. A special "1860 Retro" kit in the Victorian colours of chocolate was commissioned for the team to wear in the 2010-11 season. It was decided that a fitting start to the 2010-11 playing season would be to open the annual Cray Festival on 3 July by playing a friendly match against traditional local rivals Crockenhill F.C. at St Mary Cray Recreation Ground.

Of longer term and at least equal importance to the club, there was increasing focus upon the project to build the new ground at Sandy Lane. Will it be that the Wanderers will finally cease their wanderings? Certainly, the club had entered its 150th year in better shape than at any previous time in its long history.

Right: Mick Francis produced some brilliant drawings of Cray kits through the years for the exhibition in May 2010.

Memories 1: Nat Mercer

Nat Mercer was a Cray Wanderers player in 1888. He wrote to the 'Orpington Times' local newspaper in September 1932:

"My trial game was in 1888, a morning match for the Cray Wanderers reserve team against the Bromley first team, which we won. I was then asked to play in the first team that afternoon, versus Crouch End Vampires. Form that time I played regularly until business put a stop to Saturday sport.

There was no Kent League in those days. Our strongest opponents were Casuals, Old Westminsters (Mr Berens's old school), London Caledonians, Arsenal, Maidstone, and other Kent and military teams. I still have the old photo of the Cray Wanderers cup team 1890-91 when we were beaten 1-0 by the Royal Artillery at Sheerness in the semi-final of the Kent Junior Cup."

2: An Old Cray Wanderers Supporter

In 1932, the Orpington Times also published these memories from "an old Cray Wanderers supporter". (He did not give his name). From the players and incidents mentioned, we can date the memories to the turn of the last century, just before and after 1900.

"My first knowledge of the Wanderers was on their old ground at Derry Downs. I was invited over there from Sidcup by the late Mr Fred Collins, who was the team's indefatigable secretary for many years. I remember we went in a four-wheeled cab, and it seemed a good long drive. I am afraid I do not recollect much about the game now, but I do vividly remember that it seemed to be a matter of life and death to Collins whether the Wanderers won or lost. (I was to catch some of that enthusiasm later).

What does remain quite clear in my memory is that after the match we went to what was then, I believe, the Crays and Orpington Constitutional Club, a large house at Reynolds Cross. Here we all sat down to a meal consisting of steaks, mountains of bread and butter, and gallons of tea! We travelled home to Sidcup in the same cab, arriving there at about 10 o'clock.

Of the players that I chiefly remember, Harry Hutchins was the captain, and played at centre forward. In goal was Flower.

Jack Rogers at back had a sure kick. He was a terror to an opposing forward, and a tower of strength. Jack (if he reads this, I am sure he will forgive me) was a favourite with the lady supporters. Jack Rogers and 'Sack' Taylor the two full-backs were a tremendous asset to the club for many years.

'Kibble' Highwood at outside left was one of the nicest fellows one could wish to know – a natural gentleman and a sportsman. Feeling sometimes crept into the game (in the old Kent League days it was war to the knife!) but Highwood absolutely scorned anything that savoured of doubtful tactics.

Dover were in the Kent League, and I travelled with the team. It was arranged that we would make a weekend of it. We were quartered in a hotel. In the evening we all went to the theatre, where the farce 'The Gay Lord Quex' was playing. Those who remember this play know that Sophie Fullgarnie, the manicurist, receives an urgent telegram, and the curtain falls at the end of the second act when she is pulling up her stocking. (This was in the days of long dresses, when a lady's legs were not a free show.) This fairly finished off our fellows, and the Cray Wanderers were very nearly turned out of the theatre!

Then came the great year (1902) when the Wanderers won the Kent League. I shall never forget the day when Jack Moody scored the winning goal late in the deciding match at Sittingbourne."

Cray Wanderers FC
1860 -2010

Below: A 1930s aerial view shows part of the second Forcroft ground and also the Crays and Orpington Constitutional Club, set at an angle at Reynolds Cross.

**Cray Wanderers FC
1860 -2010**

3: Wally Heseleden

Walter 'Wally' Heselden was the old-est surviving Cray player when we spoke to him in 1983 at his home in Orchard Road.. He was 92 years old. He gave us the names of all the players in the 1910 team photograph. He recalled his memories as a Cray player in 1910. His playing career was ended when he lost a leg in the war, serving in the African desert.

"I was born in St Mary Cray in 1891. One of my earliest memories of Cray Wanderers is seeing the team return by horse and cart from a match in Eltham, singing because they had won. Also when Cray used to play against the Woolwich Arsenal, I can recall how we supporters would walk – yes, walk! – to Plumstead for the game. The walk from Cray was all across fields in those days, then along Wickham Lane to Plumstead.

I played for Southwood Athletic, a team from New Eltham. My first game for Cray Wanderers was at Belvedere in December 1910 against Prices Athletic. I became the regular left back. I replaced 'Sack' Taylor who had been the left back for many years. He lived at 'Slopers Island' – the houses off Poverest Road leading towards Carlton Parade. That side of Cray Avenue was nearly all fields. You could pick strawberries there. You could walk up to The Cricketers pub in Chislehurst Road and barely pass a building. I had some trial games for Crystal Palace F.C. and I also played for Orpington F.C. who had a sloping pitch behind the White Hart pub.

I joined the Boys Brigade at age 12 and the army at 16. I enlisted at Frances Street, Woolwich for the Chislehurst Volunteers. Work was very

Below: The Manor Ground, home of Wool-wich Arsenal FC.

scarce. The local lads from the Crays would bike around for miles looking for any casual labour. If I got a game for Cray Wanderers they gave me two shillings and sixpence for expenses. In 1912 I went to Australia where they wanted build-ers and plasterers. That put a stop to playing football, and then the war started. My medals were the Mons Star, the General Service medal and the Victory medal. I was one of the Old Contemptibles."

4: Eddie Bonwick

Eddie Bonwick wrote to us from Ottawa in Canada in 1981 when he was 80 years old, recalling his boyhood memories of Cray Wanderers. Eddie emigrated from England in July 1920. He and his wife Rose had been married for 58 years when Eddie wrote to us. "I first watched Cray Wanderers in 1910, when I was old enough to copy the other local boys and crawl under the hedge and get in 'buckshee' (free). The 'Dear Old Wands' have warmed the cockles of my heart ever since those boyhood days. We had no money so we would run across Hodsall's meadow and if we were lucky we could get through the hedge just behind the old grandstand and into the Fordcroft ground. If not, we had to wait till after half time when they let in all the kids for nothing – that's when the attend-ance really increased. If Cray had a gate of 40 shillings (£2) they were RICH.

I can vividly recall when 'Sep' Reeves took a goal-kick from the Wanderers goal and he kicked the ball clean over the visitors' goal posts at the other end, without the ball touching the ground. Other players that I remember were Bob Booker, Harry Christmas, Denis Daly, Percy Pool, Jack Smith. There were the Salmon brothers – the younger one an outstanding player. [We know that Billy Salmon scored all five goals on the day when Cray beat Wealdstone 5-2 in 1921]. The team colours, as far as I can remember were always amber and black, with stripes.

I went to school from 1905 to 1914 at Chislehurst Road school. I left to work for Mrs Nash as a general weed-picker, shoe-polisher and odd-job boy at six shillings a week. The hours were 6am till 6pm on weekdays, Saturdays till 4pm and Sundays in the mornings. I then worked at Pattullo Higgs, High Street Orpington (garden supplies, seed merchants) as a junior clerk, still on six shillings a week. Oh dear, who could ever sigh for 'The Good Old Days'! I have prospered ever since coming to Canada, and life has been good to us."

No. 5: Harry Reeves

Harry Reeves is one of the best Cray Wanderers players of all time. He starred for the team between the wars. He was capped for Kent. He was an outstanding cricketer too. He spoke to us in 1982 when we visited him and his wife Delma at their house in Goodmead Road.

"The late Arthur Collins, at the hairdressing shop in Kent Road, was a great fan of the team and he always used to introduce me to people as 'The best sportsman in the whole of Orpington!' When the Cray Wanderers won any cups and trophies he would display them in the window of his shop. He also displayed photos of old St Mary Cray.

I played football till the age of 50, and cricket till I was 65! During my twenties I became seriously ill, but I cured myself with a complete change of diet. It was sunlight food, raw with lots of vitamins. My mother was all against it, she thought I would kill myself! It was a very good team at Cray. George Miles and Frank Terry were tremendous full backs. Frank came from east London as did Harry Utz who was a charming cockney fellow. Locally there was the Banks family. Tommy Banks and all of his three brothers played for the club, and so did their nephew Tommy Allchorne who was brilliant on the wing – a very fast runner.

In my day, the five forwards all stayed up the field, and the defenders stayed back. It was much later in my career that we were taught to lie deeper and come back to fetch the ball. Even so, I don't think that I once ever tackled an opposing player! I was probably the 'greediest' player there ever was! But that was the style of football in my day, you were meant to get the ball and dribble round all the defenders, and hold on to it as long as you could!"

6: Ernie Harman

Ernie Harman ran a newsagents shop in St Mary Cray High Street after the war. He lived in Kynaston Road and was well known as a charity worker and active member of the St Mary Cray Action Group. He gave us invaluable help in compiling the history of the Cray Wanderers club. Here is a short extract from the memoir that he penned in 1976:

"My father came to St Mary Cray in 1906. As a young man in my twenties I went by the special train to see the Wands in the three finals of the Kent Amateur Cup in 1928, 1929 and 1931. We had 500 to 600 on each of those trips to Dover. I well remember the triumphant journey home in 1931 after defeating Aylesford 3-0 – we let rip with bugles, rattles, whistles, the lot! In earlier times, if the team had a long distance to go it was by horsebreak – that was more or less the only way, up until 1914.

My many good friends, from whom much information came to me, included Horace Packman (who knew the team from the 1880s), Lionel Jordan (a player before the Great War, and afterwards a professional referee), Horace Gilbert (from a whole family of loyal workers for the club) Fred Brigden (and old player and former trainer of the team), 'Shaver' Harland (who lived for the club) and Jimmy Ellard (a very keen supporter whose father played for the team)."

**Cray Wanderers FC
1860 -2010**

Left: The Crabble Athletic Grounds, home of Dover FC.

Fuming over BBC ban? Don't get mad, get even — with the Mail's cut-out-and-keep lyrics, you can belt out the Last Night of the Proms classics at home when the 'orchestral' versions are performed

RULE, BRITANNIA!

Rule, Britannia! Britannia, rule the waves!
Britons never, never, never shall be slaves.

When Britain first, at heaven's command,
Arose from out the azure main,
This was the charter of the land,
And Guardian Angels sang this strain:

(Chorus)

The nations not so blest as thee
Must, in their turn, to tyrants fall,
While thou shalt flourish great and free:
The dread and envy of them all.

(Chorus)

Still more majestic shalt thou rise,
More dreadful from each foreign stroke,
As the loud blast that tears the skies
Serves but to root thy native oak.

(Chorus)

Thee haughty tyrants ne'er shall tame;
All their attempts to bend thee down
Will but arouse thy generous flame,
But work their woe and thy renown.

(Chorus)

To thee belongs the rural reign;
Thy cities shall with commerce shine;
All thine shall be the subject main,
And every shore it circles, thine.

(Chorus)

The Muses, still with freedom found,
Shall to thy happy coasts repair.
Blest isle! with matchless beauty crowned,
And manly hearts to guard the fair.

(Chorus)

Rule, Britannia! Britannia, rule the waves!
Britons never, never, never shall be slaves.

James Thomson (1700-48)
Music by Thomas Arne (1710-78)

LAND OF HOPE AND GLORY

Dear Land of Hope, thy hope is crowned.
God make thee mightier yet!
On Sov'ran brows, beloved, renowned,
Once more thy crown is set.
Thine equal laws, by Freedom gained,
Have ruled thee well and long,
By Freedom gained, by Truth maintained,
Thine Empire shall be strong.

Land of Hope and Glory,
Mother of the Free,
How shall we extol thee,
Who are born of thee?
Wider still and wider
Shall thy bounds be set;
God, who made thee mighty,
Make thee mightier yet.

Thy fame is ancient as the days,
As Ocean large and wide:
A pride that dares, and heeds not praise,
A stern and silent pride:
Not that false joy that dreams content
With what our sires have won;
The blood a hero sire hath spent
Still nerves a hero son.

Arthur Christopher Benson (1862-1925)
Music by Edward Elgar (1857-1934)

across the world

AT least, there is still one irredeemably British quality to this year's Last Night of the Proms: Not even the finest dairy herds of Devon and Cornwall could have confected something as thick, rich and clotted as the latest solution served up by the BBC.

Instead of either ignoring the usual half-hearted complaints about 'jingoism' - a recurring grumble ahead of every Last Night since the war - or else explaining why such charges are baseless, the BBC management has, this year, just caved in.

The result is a mess that has not merely satisfied no one at all but has now managed to kickstart a national debate about the BBC itself. And it is all so needless.

Come the grand finale of this year's concert, 'Rule Britannia' will be just a shrivelled morsel. A few bars of Arne's famous anthem will be bolted on to the end of the usual medley of nautical songs - but without any words. Next comes Elgar's Pomp and Circumstance March No. 1 ('Land of Hope and Glory') but, again, minus the words.

It would have been easier for the BBC if they had simply said they were removing these pieces on a temporary basis, as indeed they did in 2001. Back then, in those dumbstruck days immediately after the 9/11 terrorist attacks in the USA, it was decided that these boisterous crowd-pleasers would hit the wrong note. So out they went, without complaint.

This time around, the BBC is floundering, meekly trying to blame this mess on the coronavirus while not denying that it has something to do with the culture wars raging beyond.

Yesterday, the director-general Lord [Tony] Hall claimed it was a 'creative conclusion' in response to Covid-19, insisting: 'It's very, very hard to have things where the whole audience normally sing along'.

This argument simply falls apart given that the song which has now overtaken Elgar - 'You'll Never Walk Alone' - is a singalong classic which *will* be sung by the guest soprano and by the BBC Singers. So, too, will 'Jerusalem' and the National Anthem.

In other words, some songs are safe to sing in a pandemic but not others. Pull the other one.

This year's guest conductor, Finland's Dalia Stasevska, 35, reportedly regards the virus as a good excuse for pruning a much-loved script. As a BBC source told the Sunday Times: 'Dalia is a big supporter of Black Lives Matter and thinks a ceremony without an audience is the perfect moment to bring change.'

Miss Stasevska has made no comment and has chosen to let this remark stand. With no substantial ethnic minorities beyond a tiny percentage of Swedes and Russians, Finland is among the least diverse societies in Europe. Finns are perhaps not best-placed to lecture the British on multiculturalism.

I suggest that Miss Stasevska has a word with her compatriot, Sakari Oramo. He was the Finnish conductor with a very difficult task - conducting the Last Night of the Proms in 2016 in the toxic aftermath of the Brexit referendum. Back then, the BBC was crippled by the same old anxieties about orgies of jingoism.

Former Proms director Nicholas Kenyon wrote darkly in the Guardian of his 'sense of foreboding that this most British of occasions might be hijacked to celebrate the triumph of Little England'.

As ever, it was nonsense - as I discovered when I went along myself. The only people who hijacked the event were an enterprising band of Remainers who had purchased a lorry load of EU flags which were given to everyone going through the door. A few Brexiteers tried to do the same with Union flags. Mr Oramo ignored it all.

Perhaps the loudest cheer of the night came when he led on his star vocalist, Peruvian tenor Juan Diego Florez, to sing Rule Britannia. Florez had come not in white tie and tails, nor dressed as Britannia. Instead, he was in the full regalia of the King of the Incas, complete with feathered cloak and Sun God helmet. The audience was ecstatic. Here was a proud Peruvian in ancient native dress, conducted by a proud Finn, leading the entire Albert Hall - plus tens of thousands gathered around the jumbo screens in Hyde Park, Glasgow and elsewhere plus millions more watching on telly - in a bravura rendition of one of Britain's best-loved tunes.

It was a perfect illustration of a point completely lost on these panicky BBC executives: the Last Night is a global event. It is also one with a healthy sense of irony - an alien concept, of course, to the woke. The thing which most sticks

---

What about other countries?

IS Rule Britannia really so offensive compared to the lyrics of other countries' hymns? Judge for yourself...

FRANCE: La Marseillaise
'They're coming right into your arms, to cut the throats of your sons, your comrades! Let's march, let's march, that their impure blood should water our fields.'

IRELAND: The Soldier's Song
'Some have come from a land beyond the wave, sworn to be free, no more our ancient sireland shall shelter the despot or the slave.'

US: The Star-Spangled Banner
The US anthem celebrates 'bombs bursting in the air' as they 'gave proof through the night that our flag was still there'. It then celebrates the spilling of 'their blood'... for 'conquer we must'.

ITALY: The Song of Italians
'The Austrian eagle has lost his plumes. This eagle that drunk the blood of Italy and Poland, together with the Cossack.'

HUNGARY: National Anthem
Remembering the Ottoman Empire as a 'barbarian nation', Hungary's anthem still includes the following suspect line about the suffering it endured at the hands of a nearby neighbour: 'the Turks' slave yoke we took upon our shoulders'.

PORTUGAL: A Portuguesa
'To march against the enemy guns! ... To arms, to arms, on land and sea!'

MEXICO: National Anthem
'War, war without truce against who would attempt to blemish the honour of the fatherland! ... The patriotic banners saturate in waves of blood.'

**Cray Wanderers FC
1860 -2010**

Founded 1860

7: Bill Golder

Mr Golder wrote to us from Bexley in 2004 with memories of Cray Wanderers F.C. getting back on their feet after the Second World War.

"I am in my 85th year and I am putting together my memoirs in case my grandsons are the least bit interested, one day!

About 1949, I along with several others was contacted by Frank Single, who asked if we would play for the Cray Wanderers. We had all played for our school in Peckham Rye during the 1930s. We had all been in the forces, and were back in civvy street.

The other players that I knew were Archie Sleafer, Merrill, Mick Golder and myself Bill Golder. Our home matches were played on a ground owned by a Nunnery in the Goddington area of Orpington. [St Philomenas were landlords of the Grassmeade pitch, next to the school in Chelsfield Lane]. Frank contacted us every week to tell us where to meet for away games. We played in the Kent Amateur League. We could never beat Footscray Social who were the best team at that time."

8: Pat White

Pat White has lived all his life in the Crays. We spoke to him in April 2010. At age 81 he had many clear memories of his happy times as a Cray Wanderers player.

"I was sixteen years old when the war ended. I had started work as a bricklayer, at the Sullivans yard. I was meant to do my national service, but they needed brickies more urgently than they needed soldiers, so I stayed put! Playing for Cray Wanderers was a natural progression really, for lads like me from the village who liked sport.

I'm afraid that we weren't a very good team just after the war. The club was in a bad state, and we had to play at the local recreation ground. We lost most of our games. Once against Sidcup United there was a big punch-up! – but I stayed at the other end of the pitch and just watched. I remember playing against Footscray on their ground at Twysdens. They were a class above us at that time.

I captained a team called Saints Athletic and we won the Sevenoaks Charity Cup. I was centre half. I started the new season 1954-55 with Cray Wanderers.
I played in the first game when we beat Welwyn Garden City 3-1 in the London League. I got a knee injury, and after that it was reserve team football for me. It cost the club ten bob to get me a knee bandage, and we travelled by coach to Barkingside, and I put the bandage on but I couldn't run properly!

Of course, I knew all the characters at the club. 'Shaver' Harland – he did everything. Mick Slater ran Bryants – the woodyard next to Orpington pond. Mick took Cray Wanderers to the new ground – it was on the church land. It wasn't a very satisfactory ground but the club had a much stronger team by then. Martin Ruddy played on the wing. When they built the pub on the new housing estate in St Paul 's Cray they named it 'The Wanderer'. Mick Slater organised all us players to go there for the opening night, when it was free pints all round!"

Right: Saints Athletic F.C. winners of the Sevenoaks Charity Cup in 1954. Archie Sleafer is on the far left in the back row. Pat White is in the front row, fourth from the left. His brother Alan 'David' White played in goal. Note that the cup is the same one that Cray Reserves won in 1896 (see page 8).

Founded 1860

9: Derek Ingram

Derek Ingram played for Cray Wanderers in 1966 and holds the record for being the first ever substitute to wear the number twelve shirt for the first team. Here he recalls helping his father, who was a stalwart on the club committee for many years.

"I will describe a typical Saturday in the 1950s when I was a boy and I would help my father Fred Ingram who was on the committee. We would leave our house in Eton Road very early in the morning. My dad would be lugging two great big wooden baskets containing all the team kit (shirts, shorts, socks) and also a bag with all the footballs. We had no car, so it was a ride on the 51 bus to the ground. When we got there, dad would start marking out the pitch. Mick Slater would have sent someone over from Bryant's yard to start the fire and get the water hot. The fire sometimes went out again, so we had to pile more wood on it.

My mum would come down and take me home after the match, treating me to fish & chips from Jane's in Carlton Parade on the way! Dad wouldn't arrive back at the house till much later, and he would bring all the kit to be washed. Mick Slater would always give him a lift in his car, because by now the kit would be very wet and muddy, and my dad couldn't possibly carry it all himself.

Then, imagine this, there were no washing-machines in those days, so there was mum in our house with five boys to bring up (I had four brothers) and the only thing to be done with the muddy and wet football kit on the Saturday night was to fill up the bath and leave it there to soak! Sunday then was "washing day". Thankfully, we had a very long garden, with enough room to hang out all the kit to dry on the line!

I can remember the ground at Fordcroft [1951 to 1954]. I remember my father telling me that when the very first game was played there, the referee found that loads of flint had come to the surface, so he wouldn't let the players kick-off until people had gone out on to the pitch to remove it all. There were always problems there – the pitch was sited very close to the River Cray and the ground became very wet in the winter. My father told me that when Cray Wanderers had built the ground there, they had diverted the path of the river, to make more room for the football pitch! There were local farmers on the committee, so they supplied the necessary tractors and diggers. When the waterway authorities found out what had happened, they wrote to the club and demanded rectification, but it didn't matter because the Wands were already moving away. The church had said that they needed the land.

After that, Cray Wanderers played at Grassmeade in Chelsfield Lane. I vividly remember the game in 1959 when the All Stars Television team played a team of mostly local Cray players. A huge crowd came to watch. Tommy Steele and lots of other big names in showbiz were playing, and I got all their autographs."

Far Left: Derek Ingram with his father, Fred.

Left: Tommy Steele alongside Cray's Reg Davies at Grassmeade in 1959.

Cray Wanderers FC 1860 -2010

Founded 1860

The Hall of Fame

From the 150 years of Cray Wanderers history 1860 to 2010 we are proud to single out these very special personalities – each and every one of them most deservedly holding a place in the club's "Hall of Fame".

1: Harry Hutchins

Harry Hutchins is the first example of a true local hero in the history of Cray Wanderers – a veritable "Harry Hotspur". He was the team captain and the centre forward during the 1890s. He was a well-known and poplar local tradesman too.

In 1932, a supporter wrote: "I believe the team would have died for Harry. Apart from the fine game he played – crafty, bustling, sure and entirely unselfish – he had that great gift of inspiring in others the doggedness that knows not defeat until the whistle goes for 'time'. Many an apparent lost game have I seen turned into victory by the unquenchable optimism of the Wanderers skipper. No wonder his team loved him! His smile disarmed them. Of all those who mourned his untimely death in the terrible disaster at Handcross in 1906, none could have been more sincere than his old colleagues at the Cray Wanderers club."

2: Herbert Berens

The Berens family lived at Kevington Manor. They were big landowners in the Crays. There is no doubt that their patronage of Cray Wanderers F.C. helped to establish the team as a senior force in county football. Up until the mid-1880s Cray had been a small-time village football team, but once the Berens family brought their influence to bear, the club grew in stature.

Herbert Berens was a star player – a forward - in the Cray Wanderers team. He had played for Westminster School. The locals referred to him as 'Mr 'Bert Berens'. He was manager of his father's estate. He died from pneumonia at the tragically early age of thirty, in 1896. There was a huge turnout at his funeral. He is buried at All Saints Church in Orpington just a few yards away from the Bromley Museum.

3: George 'Shaver' Harland

No history of Cray Wanderers F.C. would be complete without highlighting George Harland's uniquely long and loyal service to the club. He was a local man and an outstanding sportsman.

George first played for the Wands in 1910. He was a left-sided player, but during a period of almost twenty years he reputedly played in every single position for the team at one time or another. Long after he was supposed to have retired, he would turn out when the team was one short. He once even played in goal, and Cray won the match two-nil! Not content with that, after the matches George would swap his football shirt for his bandsman's uniform and would play the cornet for

Right: Herbert Berens (left) and Harry Hutchins.

Far right: George 'Shaver' Harland.

G. P. HARLAND, 11, POPLAR TERRACE, (our Trainer), is open for engagements at Dances, Public or Private, with his new up-to-date Drum Set.

the Cray brass band that traditionally provided the after-match entertainment at one of the local public houses.

Eddie Bonwick told us: "George Harland lived in the same row of houses as I did – at Station Road cottages, St Mary Cray. After his playing days were over he loved running up and down the touchlines shouting out 'Play up the Wands.' This always enthused the crowds".

'Shaver's many roles at Cray Wanderers after the war included trainer, secretary and groundsman. He always had a cheery smile for everyone.

4: Mick Slater

Were it not for Mick Slater, there would be no Cray Wanderers today. Mick stepped in to rescue the club when it was struggling badly in 1950. A native of Bermondsey and Deptford, he had moved to Orpington where he managed the Bryants woodyard. He started up and ran the Cray Tigers speedway cycle team with great success at Northfield Farm after the war. On this sport going out of fashion,

he turned his attention to football and he persuaded some other local businessmen to invest in the ailing Cray Wanderers club.

During the next twenty-four years Mick became known as "Mr Cray Wanderers". He transformed the club. The team became extremely successful in the London League, the Aetolian League, the Metropolitan League and the county cups. Mick thought up several publicity stunts to put Cray Wanderers on the map. He staged floodlight football matches at Grassmeade in 1953 when no one else in the country was doing it. He had a tremendous work ethic and he campaigned tirelessly to bring better sports and social facilities to the Crays, especially to occupy the local youths and help keep them out of trouble.

Mick overcame many hurdles in his battle to upgrade Cray Wanderers on and off the field. He found and built them a new ground on the corner of Cray Avenue and Kent Road in 1951. Three years later he obtained the use of Grassmeade where he improved the construction sufficiently well for county representative matches to be played there. It was a huge blow to Mick when the owners decided to sell the land and build houses there. One of Mick's last acts before his death in 1974 was to negotiate a deal with Sid-

Left: *Martin Ruddy (left) with Mick Slater.*

Cray Wanderers FC 1860 -2010

Founded 1860

cup Conservative Club so that Cray Wanderers could move to a new ground at Oxford Road in 1973, on the outskirts of Footscray. The stand there is named the Mick Slater Stand.

5: Ken Collishaw

Ken Collishaw holds the club record for the highest total of goals scored by one player. He was an outstanding centre forward. He netted 274 goals while playing for Cray Wanderers from 1954 to 1964. He twice scored seven goals in a game, and he scored in eight consecutive games. These are club records too.

Ken was renowned for being a very direct, bustling and competitive player. He could head the ball like a bullet, and shoot with both feet. Cray were prolific goalscorers during the 1960s when Micky Thompson partnered Ken in the forward line. Micky wore the number 10 shirt and netted exactly 100 goals for Cray. Another popular forward for Cray was Johnny Stevens on the left wing. His crosses provided many of the goals, and he was deadly from penalty-kicks too.

Cray have had some other good centre forwards wearing the number 9 shirt in the post-war years. Bill Bedwell scored a century of goals in the 1950s. Local lad Barry Diggins took over from Collishaw and made a name for himself. John Duffy, Butch Dunn and Phil Williams were stars for Cray at Oxford Road in the 1970s and 1980s, where another big goalscorer was the small but outstandingly

MONDAY, 29th APRIL, 1957				K.O. 6.30 p.m.
WINGATE	-	-	-	Blue & White

L. Mydatt

2 B. Beharrier   3 D. Dryer

4 M. Black   5 L. Warren   6 S. Burns

7 L. Sollof   8 J. Silver   9 R. Phillips   10 A. Tapper   11 L. Coleman

Referee : Mr. H. V. Kent   Linesmen : Mr. G. J. Kimber
                                             Mr. K. Mortimore

11 M. Ruddy   10 A. Basham   9 K. Collishaw   8 L. Butterfill   7 S. Talbot

6 R. Allen   5 J. Day   4 H. Wager

3 R. Davis   2 L. Rawle

H. Pocock

CRAY WANDERERS	-	-	Amber & Black

skilful Dave Waight. In the 1990s, the powerful Phil Collins and Tunde Utsaja smashed in lots of goals for Cray. In the new Millennium, the brothers Jamie and Lewis Wood have scored 100 and 50 goals respectively for the club.

6: John Dorey

John Dorey is believed to hold the club record for the player who has played the most games for Cray Wanderers.

John played 500 times for Cray while he was centre half and captain from 1961 to 1971. A polished centre half, he led by example and was an outstandingly skilful player. These were the

Right: At The White Hart, Orpington in 1966. Left to right: John Dorey, Ernie Smith, Barry Diggins, Albert Dorey, Alan Howe, Ray Hutchins and Howard Styles, with Derek Ingram seated at the front.

golden years for Cray at Grassmeade. The team won several trophies. Some of the best remembered players from this time were the full backs Peter Clark and Alan Howe, the classy Ray Hutchins at half back, Tex Wiltshire in midfield, and John Faulkner a defender who went on to play for Leeds United and Luton Town.

It is notable that some of Cray's best post-war captains have been centre-halves. Joe Harris in the 1950s was also a county cap, like John Dorey. Phil Emblen was Cray's "Captain Courageous" in the 1970s when the team was nicknamed "Biddle's Battlers" in honour of their manager Johnny Biddle. Cray's current centre half and captain is Mark Willy, a strong-tackling player and a fine leader who has taken the Wands into the Ryman Premier League and will undoubtedly be rated as one of the club's best players of all time.

7: Gary Hillman

It has been a spectacular success story of "onwards and upwards" for Cray Wanderers since Gary Hillman took over as chairman in 1994.

Generous financial support was received from Hillman & Son (Building Contractors) to get the club back on its feet after a number of setbacks in the early 1990s. In more recent years, John Woolf as vice-chairman has provided further generous support that has helped to keep the momentum going.

Under the chairmanship of Gary Hillman the Cray Wanderers have progressively raised their profile in the local community, including the establishment of youth football teams at all ages from Under-7s upwards. The Wands have partnered too with the Coopers Technology College in Chislehurst, to start a very successful football academy.

Cray Wanderers have announced a plan to build a new football ground at Sandy Lane in 2014. If successful, this will re-establish the club in the heartland of the Crays where it originated 150 years ago. Since 1998 the first team been has playing its home matches at Bromley F.C. in Hayes Lane , under a temporary ground-sharing arrangement.

Gary Hillman is driving the ambitious project that will not only provide a new football pitch for Cray Wanderers in Sandy Lane but will incorporate a range of new health, sport and leisure facilities, and a hundred new jobs, all for the benefit of the local community.

8: Ian Jenkins

Ian Jenkins is the current manager of Cray Wanderers. He is the most successful manager in the club's history. Since his appointment in 1999, Cray have won the Kent League championship twice, and also the Kent League Cup and the Kent Senior Trophy. The club was duly promoted into the Ryman League in 2004. After five progressive years in Division One they gained promotion into the Ryman Premier when they won the play-offs in 2008-09. This means that in the year 2010, the club's 150th anniversary, Cray Wanderers are playing at their highest level of football in their entire history.

Ian first came to Cray as a player in 1993. He holds a personal record of scoring at least one goal for the team in fifteen consecutive seasons. Ian was captain of the Cray team that won the Kent Senior Trophy in 1993. Sam Wright scored the winning goal for Cray in the final at the Priestfield Stadium, the home of Gillingham FC. Ten years later in Cray's memorable "double double" season of 2002-03, Ian and Sam were managers of the Cray first team and reserve team who each won the Kent League championship and the League Cup.

Ian has been ably assisted by his management team of Joe Francis and Paul Blade while achieving such outstanding success for Cray Wanderers.

Below: *Ian Jenkins in 1997.*

Chapter 8 – Letters to the Club

**Cray Wanderers FC
1860 -2010**

Cray Wanderers were delighted to receive a pennant from FC Barcelona which had been signed by the team. The pennant is proudly displayed by Stephen McCartney (top) and John McArthur in the images right.

A letter from the club accompanying the pennant is reproduced below, and is without doubt the most prestigious communication received by the club in 150 years.

A further letter was received from the London F.A. who clearly understood the enormous importance of the anniversary for the establishing of football in the south of the country. Few clubs can claim to pre-date the formation of their parent association!

FCBARCELONA

President

Mr. Gary Hillman
President
Cray Wanderers FC
46-48 Ennersdale Road
London SE13 6JB
ENGLAND

Dear President,

In my name and on behalf of the FC Barcelona Board of Directors, I would like to express our most sincerest congratulations for your 150th anniversary.

It gives me great pleasure to wish you a great success in the organization of the events that you will engage for your anniversary.

Receive our congratulations and our sincere good wishes,

JOAN LAPORTA I ESTRUCH

Barcelona, 18th February 2010

LONDON FOOTBALL ASSOCIATION LIMITED

Gary Hillman
Chairman
Cray Wanderers Football Club
c/o 46-48 Ennersdale Road
London
SE13 6JB

Dear Gary

Re: Cray Wanderers Football Club 150th anniversary

On behalf of the Association I write to congratulate the club on its incredible achievement on reaching its 150th year. Only Sheffield FC has managed this so you in a unique club of two!

As the oldest club in London we feel particularly proud. Your achievement is extra special because while London has a number of professional clubs, the capitals unique land values has resulted in so many senior clubs disappearing particularly in recent years. It is a tribute to the club, and you Gary, that this extraordinary anniversary has been reached.

With very best regards

D G Fowkes
Chief Executive

Cray Wanderers have never owned their own ground, although the hope is that the club will move to their own newly-built ground in 2014. Over the past 150 years the club have played at ten grounds, and another ground was planned but never built. Other than Hayes Lanes, six miles west, the ground locations are shown in the map below.

**Cray Wanderers FC
1860 -2010**

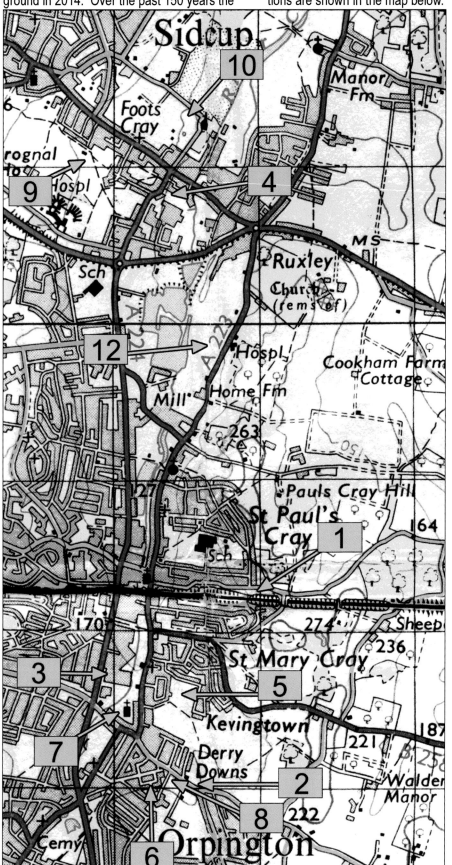

1: Star Lane 1860 onwards
2: Derry Downs pre 1880s - 1898
3: Fordcroft 1998 - 1936
4: Twysdens 1936 - 1940
5: St Mary Cray Rec: 1948 - 1951
6: Northfield Farm 1950 - 1951
7: Fordcroft (2) 1951 - 1954
8: Grassmeade 1943 - 1948
              & 1953 - 1973
9: Oxford Road 1973 - 1998
10: Rectory Road proposed 1990
11: Hayes Lane 1998 - 2014?
12: Sandy Lane: from 2014?

Cray Wanderers FC 1860 -2010

Founded 1860

Right: The approximate location of Star Lane can be seen, and with a tennis court still noted the area clearly was still a place where sports were played. Map dated 1896.

1: Star Lane

Records now lost stated that the club first played on a field in Star Lane, and although it is believed this was where the cemetery was later established it is now impossible to accurately locate the ground.

As the club was established by railway workers who would probably have been accomodated near to the line they were building it is likely that their sporting activities took place nearby.

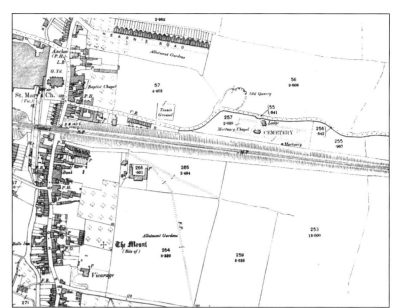

2: Derry Downs

The lack of primary sources means that we cannot accurately pinpoint the location of ground where Cray Wanderers played immediately before moving to Fordcroft in 1898, nor the date they ceased playing at Star Lane.

in 1976 Ernie Harman wrote: 'Over the years it has been said many times to me why did not Cray Wanderers buy the Fordcroft ground. Horace Gilbert told me that why the Wanderers left Grassmeade before World War One was that the ground was taken as open land and the public watched the football free. The committeee decided to ask Mr Joynson whose land it was if they could take admission money. Mr Joynson

offered a piece of land at Fordcroft which he owned, so they could take admission and Cray moved there in 1898.

The preface to a small booklet published in 1951 of the Cray Wanderers FC history by Mick Slater stated: 'By 1883 the club occupied the site which is now called Grassmeade, it was then a recreation ground'.

A match report of December 1886 refers to 'the Recreation Ground at St Mary Cray' but it is unclear as to whether this is the current Rec. Maps of the time give no indication of exactly where the Derry Downs ground was.

3: Fordcroft

A wooden grandstand which stood at Derry Downs was moved by horse and cart to the new ground, named after the small hamlet nearby.

The ground was on flat ground by the river Cray, but on the opposite bank to the village. It would appear that access was by a bridge and footpath at a weir on the High Street, seen in the map left. A walk along the same route today is still possible but the changes of the last seventy years have seen a rural scene change to one of suburban industry.

Below: The enclosed ground at Fordcroft is on two adjoining maps in 1909 which have been joined to show the ground in its full glory. It is not clear where the official entrance was but the footpaths and bridge over the river suggests it was in the south east corner.

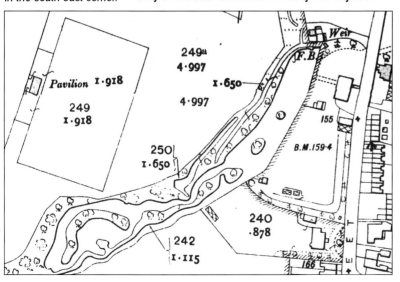

The land on which the ground was developed was owned by Mr. Joynson, who had a nearby paper mill which printed the bank notes for the Bank of England. It was possible to enclose the ground and so charge a gate for the first time, although the boundary fencing was probably not much more than the old field hedge.

Few images have survived to give much detail about the ground, although a number of team groups were taken over the years in an open area by the pitch to the south of the stand.

From these it is possible to deduce that the stand was home-made but with a good elevated position, albeit with four stanchions partly blocking the view. Bench seats were provided in ten rows, which with the three bays gives a capacity of between 500 and 600.

Early photos show a staircase at the rear, but with this being blocked up in later images it is not clear how fans then accessed the stand.

The construction of the Orpington by-pass in the 1930s completely changed the character of the Cray valley, and all of a sudden the land became valuable for industrial development. As previously mentioned the land was sold and the Tip Top bakery built over the ground, now itself a listed building.

No aerial photos have been located although it is known that an open air Olympic sized swimming pool opened adjacent to the ground in the 1930s called Blue Lagoon (now Lagoon Road), and an aerial image of that is known to exist. It is hoped that if located this image may also feature Fordcroft in the background. Efforts continue to be made to track this image down but sadly were not successful in time for the publication of this book.

***Left**: A few photos of groups taken at Fordcroft have survived, all of which show the southern end of the stand. Here a group of club officials are pictured.*

***Left**: The stand at Fordcroft is seen behind a Cray Reserves line-up in 1922, by which time the side staircase has been removed.*

***Left**: Using visual evidence from the photos in the club archive along with details of the dimensions of the stand from maps it has been possible to reconstruct the appearance opf the stand using computer graphics. Sadly it would seem that no-one who saw a game at the ground is alive now to confirm the accuracy of the image. Image: Courtesy of Ian Midgley.*

Cray Wanderers FC
1860 -2010

Right: The Twysdens ground in Footscray. Map dated 1939.

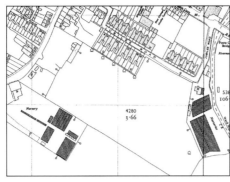

Twysdens

Cray moved north to share with Footscray Social F.C. when Fordcroft was lost. Footscray Social Club Trustee Terry Waller says: 'The old ground was on Twysdens Meadows which is now the site of the Coca Cola car park. The entrance to the ground was through gates situated where the entrance to the car park for the houses, opposite the Cray Road entrance to the Club today'. The houses in what was Jubilee Road in the photo on page 23 indicate the location of the pitch.

St Mary Cray Recreation Ground

The rec in St Mary Cray provided another simple home, but as it was not enclosed no gate could be taken. A simple overhang from the changing room block gave some cover, but being set at an angle to the pitch was far from ideal.

Right: Action from a home game for AF.C. Egerton in the Kent County League Premier Division in 1997. Photo: Mike Floate.

The area remains in use for foootball today and was the home ground of AF.C. Egerton in the Kent County League in the 1990s.

The changing room block also survives but the cover has been removed. At the time of writing there are plans for the building to be renovated to again enable football of a more senior level to be played at the ground.

*Right: By 2006 the changing rooms have seen better days but will hopefully soon be renovated and back in use.
Photo: Mike Floate.*

When opened the rec had open fields alongside, another indication of how rural St Mary Cray was even within living memory.

*Right: St Mary Cray Recreation ground showing the football pitch and the changing rooms in the 1930s.
Postcard from the Mike Floate archive.*

RECREATION GROUND, ST MARY CRAY.

Northfield Farm

For one season Cray played on a ground at Northfield, since developed for housing. The pitch was in the middle of the track in the map, and is now covered by Northfield Avenue and Sussex Avenue. The ground was a simple stop-gap venue but as it was enclosed a gate could be taken. Grassmeade was immediately adjacent to the ground.

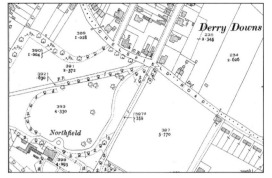

__Left__: North-field in 1933.

__Below__: Fordcroft / Tothills is the irregularly shaped field, map dated 1933.

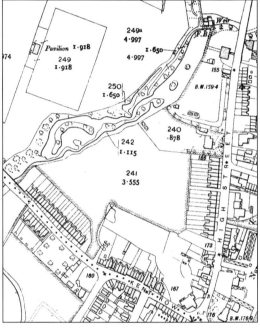

Fordcroft / Tothills

Another ground was quickly developed on an open area between the river and the High Street, just across from the pre-war Fordcroft ground whose name this ground adopted. A brook running down the slope being channelled so the pitch could be laid out. A simple cover was built from scaffolding and covered a simple bank of seats. A tea hut was situated adjacent, and judging by the slope in the photo would appear to be on the south side of the ground. It was probably for the best that the land was eventually required for the building of a church as the ground often flooded. Much of the area is now open ground on the riverside path.

Cray Wanderers FC
1860 -2010

Founded 1860

<u>*Right*</u>: *The location of Grassmeade and the housing covering Northfield can be seen in this map from 1959.*

Grassmeade

<u>*Below*</u>: *Grassmeade in 1970.*
Photo: Aerofilms

With the move to Grassmeade it seemed at last that Cray had found a ground with potential for development which could enable them to move up to higher leagues.

The ground was already an established football ground with a railed pitch and changing rooms, as can be seen in the photo on page 100.

The close proximity of St Philomenas School can also be seen, who as owners caused the loss of the ground in selling it for housing. Killewarren Road now covers the site of the ground.

The original changing rooms were retained and flanked by low concrete terracing. The whole length was covered and included the area in

front of the changing rooms which had luxurious former airliner seating installed.

At the western end of this side was a spacious clubhouse. The pitch was railed all round although other than on the clubhouse side there was no terracing. Fans watching from the far side at times had to keep an eye on proceedings behind them as a hockey pitch meant that an occasional stray ball could strike an unsuspecting spectator on the ankle. Knowing Cray fans' colourful use of language I am sure that those around would have been well entertained at such times!

In a letter to the *Kentish Times* in 1969, headed 'Goodbye to Grassmeade?', supporter Mr D. Littlewood struck a lyrical note when he wrote: "Take a look at the setting - the large chestnut tree in one corner, and the tall trees behind the Northfield Avenue goal; and is it only my imagination that the trees seem to nod approval when Cray score a goal, and shake their heads in sorrow when Cray lose?"

Left & Bottom Left: *Grassmeade before and after Cray left the ground in 1973.*
Photos: Bob Lilliman.

**Cray Wanderers FC
1860 -2010**

Left: *The 1950 Kent Junior Cup Semi-Final sees Bakers Sports winning 5-0 at Grassmeade against Borough Green FC.*
Photo: Darren Fisher / http://www.plattunited.co.uk/

Left: *Cray v Charlton Athletic A in 1960.*
Photo: Ian Fordyce.

Below: *The airliner seats in front of the changing room. In the foreground, Tex Wiltshire (left) and John Dorey. In the background is John Faulkner who went on to play for Leeds United and Luton Town. The spectator is Ernie 'Doc' Smith, the club Chairman.*

**Cray Wanderers FC
1860 -2010**

Founded 1860

**Right**: _Oxford Road in the 1950s. The pitch ran alongside what was then a bowling green._

**Right**: _Plans submitted in 1972 for a turnstile block._

**Below**: _The plans submitted to Bexley Council in 1972._
Both plans courtesy of Bexley Local Studies and Archive Centre.

7: Oxford Road

Shortly before his untimely death Mick Slater found what he hoped would be a temporary home for Cray a few miles to the north in Sidcup, overlooking the Cray valley.

The club submitted a planning application in which they sought to build a heavily-engineered roof extending to the touchline which was refused. At the same time floodlights were included on the drawing, a problem which would still confront the club almost thirty years later.

The ground was owned by the local Conservative Club and no bar could be included, limiting the options for making money to run and develop the club.

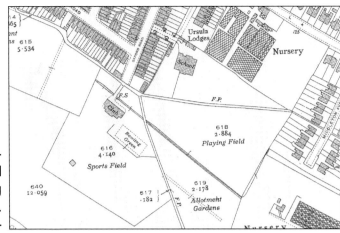

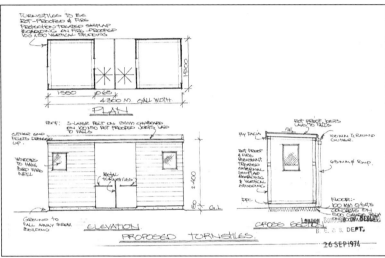

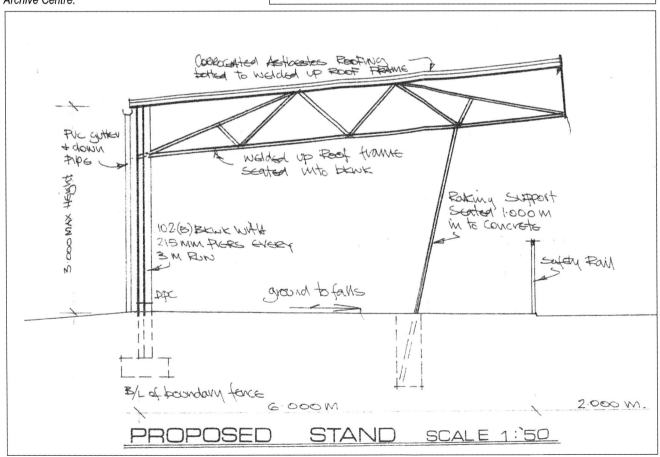

The northern side of the ground at Oxford Road by the entrance was the location of the planned stand. The simplified structure agreed by Bexley Council was begun soon after the club moved in but work stopped with the roof complete but with the concrete terracing only extending half way. Mike Floate recalls: 'On my first visit to the ground solid bags of cement were to be seen strewn among the rubble as if the workers had vanished due to a sudden downpour.

The terraces were a popular place to stand and the usual Cray wit made for entertainment even if the football was poor.

The stand remained in this incomplete state for over twenty years until the concrete was extended and bright red tip-up seats were installed along two thirds of the length to satisfy Kent League grading requirements.

The structure of the stand survived the relative neglect of the ground being used only for reserve team football but the local youths could not resist the chance of vandalising the seats and using the brickwork as a canvas. The stand presented a sorry impression in 2008.

One lasting memory of the ground was the slope, clearly seen my photos of the ground.'

Cray Wanderers FC
1860 -2010

Top left: The half-built stand at Oxford Road is filled in this undated view from the club archives.

Left: Two views of the stand as completed to satisfy Kent League ground grading requirements, and ten years later with the seats removed.
Photos: Mike Floate.

Below: Two panoramic views of the Oxford Road ground from both ends.
Photos: Mike Floate.

Cray Wanderers FC
1860 -2010

Founded 1860

Top right: *The turnstile block in the m id 1990s.*

Right: *The bank behind the goal at the Sidcup end provided an excellent place from which to watch the game, seen here in 2006.*

Right: *On the south side of the ground two simple covers were erected in the 1990s and were remarkably still standing in 2006. Photos: Mike Floate.*

Team coach John Dunbar produced two issues of a fanzine entitled 'What Slope?' in 1994. The name reflected an in-joke that the Wands commit-tee would always deliberately deny the steepness of the hill, when visiting players and officials first saw the pitch and gasped in horror!

Ted Palmer, a Cray supporter now living in Sussex, has a special affection for this ground, for he grew up in Sidcup before the war, and attended the school in Oxford Road. (It is still there).

Many of the older supporters have told us of the old "tin hut" that was the social club preceding the present day Cons Club, and Ted has added the memory that the allotments behind the entrance and car park at the football ground are standing on land that was flattened by wartime bombing.

Phil Williams is Ted's favourite and best-remem-bered player from the Wands' playing days at Oxford Road.

Rectory Lane

Back in 1990 an excellent local football fan-zine 'Football Utopia' published by Chris Munns detailed ambitious plans for a new ground planned by Cray Wanderers. Located at Rectory Road, down Sidcup Hill in Footscray not far from their Oxford Road ground, the promise of covered terraces and a big stand backed up the stated aim of eventually competing locally with Welling United.

The downturn in the national economy caused a

hasty reappraisal when the money behind the ven-ture failed to materialise and the club continued to play at Oxford Road for a further eight seasons.

Right: *The plans for the ground at Rectory Lane provided by the club to Chris Munns for use in the 'Football Utopia' fanzine.*

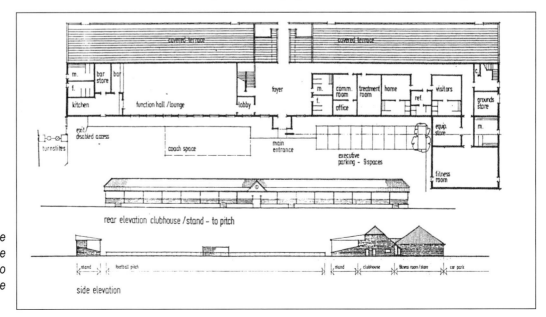

Return to St Mary Cray Recreation Ground

The first fixture in Cray's 150th Anniversary celebrations was held back in St Mary Cray, with local rivals Crockenhill F.C. as the opponents. The pitch on the far side away from the changing room block was used and a crowd of approaching 500 attended. Local residents turned out in force along with many groundhoppers, including Duncan Mackay and John Miller who flew from Scotland for the game.

Left & below: A crowd again gathers to enjoy a football match on St Mary Cray Recreation Ground, July 3rd 2010.
Photos: Mike Floate.

Hayes Lane

In 1998 the Kent League required grounds to have floodlights. A groundshare was agreed with Bromley F.C. at Hayes Lane, which still serves as a home ground at the time of writing. The excellent terraces on three sides provided a suitably historic backdrop for the friendly fixture against Leyton Orient in July 2010.

Below: Hayes Lane.
Photo: Mike Floate.

Cray Wanderers FC
1860 -2010

Founded 1860

Sandy Lane

In 2010 it was announced that Cray Wanderers FC wanted to build a new eco-friendly stadium in St Mary Cray. The intention was to develop a ground to Conference standards, incorporating a range of health and leisure facilities such as 5-a-side football pitches, a fitness centre, academy, nursery and club shop.

In an interview with the *News Shopper*, club chairman Gary Hillman said: 'It will be a massive boost for the local area. Not only will we create new jobs but we'll give the area a renewed sense of pride. We feel it's an ideal location for a type of sporting village.'

The area around the estimated £10m development in Sandy Lane is already home to a dry ski-slope, golf course and fishing lakes.

At the time of writing the club is working towards submitting a full planning application and be ready to move in for the start of the 2014/15 season. Local support is getting behind the plans to bring Cray Wanderers FC back home to the Crays.

Chapter 9 – The Charity Ball

A Charity Ball at Oakley House in Bromley was the first of a series of special events that took place in 2010 to mark the 150th anniversary of Cray Wanderers FC.

Attended by 350 people on 5th June, the function was a great success. Over £15,000 was raised for the local Bromley Y charity which is an independent charity that supports young people in the London Borough of Bromley.

**Cray Wanderers FC
1860 -2010**

__Left__: Back row (L to R): Darren Anslow, Martin Barnard, Colin Ball Front: George Porter, Jack Parkinson

__Left__: Gary Hillman with the Bromley Y ladies.

Wands' magic gesture for charity

FOOTBALL

ONE of the world's oldest football clubs has demonstrated its strong community links with a major charity donation.

Cray Wanderers Football Club raised £15,000 for the Bromley Y charity at their 150th anniversary ball at Oakley House in Bromley.

Founded in 1860, Cray are the second oldest football club in the world and the charity ball was one of several special events that the Wands are organising in 2010 to mark their proud 150-year history. Chairman Gary

Hillman said: "More than 350 people enjoyed a splendid evening celebrating the 150th year of Cray Wanderers and I am delighted that we were able to raise such a large sum of money to help Bromley Y to continue its important work for the young people of the Bromley borough."

Bromley Y is an independent charity that provides free and confidential counselling to young people aged 11 to 23. It also runs parent support groups, anti-bullying workshops, alcohol abuse, drama and art therapy groups and family planning.

CHARITY BALL: Cray chairman Gary Hillman with charity staff.

**Cray Wanderers FC
1860 -2010**

*__Right__: Mr Alan Turvey
(Chairman & President of
the Ryman League) and
his wife Margaret.*

*__Right__: Wendy, Sarah
and Jo.*

*__Far Right__: George Porter,
Ian Jenkins, Mark Willy,
Leigh Bremner and Gary
Hillman on stage for the
2009-10 player of the
season presentations.*

*__Right__: John Dorey and
Stan Matthews from the
1962-63 team.*

An exhibition of 150 years of Cray Wanderers F.C. history was staged at the London Borough of Bromley Museum during May and June 2010.

The display was featured on television in the GMTV London News programme on 22 May. This can be viewed at: www.itv.com/london/cray-day90665/

Cray Wanderers would like to thank Marie-Louise Kerr (Curator) and Christine Alford (Assistant) for all their advice and encouragement that made the exhibition such a big success.

Thanks are also due to Danny Pape, a student from west London, whose short film 'It's A Wanderful Life' is an entertaining portrayal of the origins and history of Cray Wanderers. Danny visited us on 6 March 2010 to film some locations in St Mary Cray, followed by action from the Wands home match versus Wealdstone in the Ryman Premier League. Danny's film can be viewed at:
www.youtube.com/watch?v=do2KanfXsGA

A big highlight of the exhibition was a display of the original medals won by Frank Terry, who played for the Wands between the wars. We are most grateful to the Terry family for kindly lending us the medals and helping us to feature the career of one of Cray's best-ever players.

**Cray Wanderers FC
1860 -2010**

*Left: Ian Fordyce.
Photo: Trevor Mulligan.*

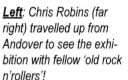

Left: Chris Robins (far right) travelled up from Andover to see the exhibition with fellow 'old rock n'rollers'!

Left: Allen Bishop with his wife Jean and members of his family, recalling Allen's days as a Cray player during the 1960s.

Cray Wanderers FC 1860 -2010

Founded 1860

Here is a selection of the many comments that visitors wrote in the Guest Book at the Cray Wanderers F.C. 150 exhibition.

What a fantastic exhibition. Well done the Cray Wanderers F.C. and Bromley Museum for putting this together. A real celebration of local football, and working-class culture. Bravo! John Pateman. *Superb exhibition – so much history and so many memories. I loved the photo of Grassmeade.* Gary Defrond.

Great exhibition. Can't wait to bring my grandsons. Alan Basham. *Good to see the support that you still have.* Iris Pendergast. *Fantastic tribute. Congratulations … here's to the next 150 years.* Colin Heys.

Excellent - pure nostalgia! Well done. Alan Williams (Gravesend). *Great display, nice to see pictures of Dave Jackson, my dad.* Lorraine Cowin. *One does look different after fifty years.* Reg Davies – ex-Cray player. *I came with my grandad Allen Bishop, who played for Cray Wanderers when he was fifteen years old!* Amy Richardson.

Good to see so many great memories. Excellent show. There were some outstandingly good players at Cray when I played in the 1950s. Martin Ruddy on the wing, Johnny Day in defence, Ken Collishaw at centre forward. Mick Slater ran the club - he always made sure that the players were looked after. Terry Nicholls.

Brought back many happy memories of going to Grassmeade in Chelsfield Lane with my dad. The display of old programmes was great, and to get a signed pennant and letter from A.F.C. Barcelona shows what one football club means to another. Mark Jarman. *Just what I needed, a quiet meander, inspired by the past. Many thanks.* Hazel Copland.

A good selection of photos old and new. Good luck for the future. Chris Daniels, supporter 44 years. *Great exhibition. Cray was the first 'proper' football match that I ever went to (over forty years ago – I still remember it like it was yesterday!).* Paul Ashford.

Excellent display – Harry would have loved it! Nice to see so many familiar names, bringing back memories of the happiest years. Harry was the best centre forward and manager, but then I'm biased! Cheryl Richardson.

My dad Jumbo Collins played in the late 1930s – nice to see a picture of him at the exhibition. It all brought back many happy memories of my childhood. S Hunt (Dartford). *Looking back at old memories of Cray Wanderers. I used to play at Grassmeade for about five to six seasons, then they had to move to Oxford Road. My two uncles played as well – in 1938 Horace*

Collins (Jumbo) and Alf Collins. Lovely memories. Ron Wissenden.

Very, very good display. Roll on 2014! Colin Smart, Vice-President, Orpington, Bromley & District Sunday Football League. *Been going to Cray since the Grassmeade days. Good football played just how it should be. Come on you Wands! PS: Patsy Carey was a wizard!* Paul Younger.

Great presentation, especially to see the names of the late 1970s and early 1980s: Phil Emblen, Tony Pamphlett, Susso, Dave Waight, and my nightmare to mark, Kevin Walsh. Colin Ball ex-player of Alma Swanley; and parents Phil Ball & Marilyn Ball.

Really enjoyed the exhibition. Great work in putting it all together. Great memories. I saw my first Cray match in 1948 with my dad. Doug Head. *A fantastic achievement to reach 150 years. Good luck for the next 150!* Colin Head, (I'm a Bromley fan!).

First watched Cray at the second 'Fordcroft' ground, sometimes known as 'Tothills', in 1951. Saw every home match for the next fifteen years, before moving away. Still have all the programmes – many hundreds, in an old cardboard box. Best player – Ken Collishaw, by a mile; but also for sheer class, Johnny Day. Oh, what memories this exhibition has brought back. Well done to all those who put it on, and to all those people working to get the club back to Cray. Royston Bond.

Very impressive, nicely exhibited. Well done. E.W.W. (Millwall F.C. historian). *Brings back many happy memories of my own clubs (Darenth Heathside, Furness and Slade Green) and the many tussles with Cray from the 1960s into the 2000s. A well put-together exhibition. Well done.* Martin Wiseman.

Must pay tribute to the late great Mick Slater and his wonderful wife Harriet who did so much for the club. Mick worked very hard to help the club grow. Neil Denny. *Wonderful exhibition – look forward to the new ground.* Dave Reed. *Excellent exhibition. Look forward to seeing Cray Wanderers at the new ground.* Bob Lilliman.

Frank Terry was a very good player. He had chances to play for Charlton Athletic. He moved from East Ham to Cray, he met Betty and they were married. Betty did the sandwiches and teas for the Cray players. I know this because I am the daughter, Jean. I was always up at the ground. He was a smashing dad. Jean Terry.

A really good exhibition – well done and best of luck for the next 150 years! Cllr. David McBride.

Come back to Cray! Paul Ashford.

Cray kicked off their 2010-11 playing season with a special invitation match against Crockenhill FC. In the souvenir programme, the Wands chairman Gary Hillman wrote: 'Cray Wanderers F.C. is delighted to be staging this special fixture against our friends and old local rivals Crockenhill F.C. here at St Mary Cray recreation ground.

The records show that the very first football matches played by the Wanderers were at Star Lane and then at Derry Downs. Local village sides or army teams would have provided the opposition in those early days. In 1898, the Wands moved a few hundred yards to the far side of the River Cray to play at Fordcroft.

These were times of change and growth for Cray Wanderers. County football had become properly organised. League and cup competitions had started. In 1895 the club adopted its present-day amber & black colours. The original shirts were chocolate.

However, the match today between Cray Wanderers and Crockenhill is not only about the past; it is symbolic of the future, too.

This afternoon will be the first time in nearly forty years that the Wands have played a football match in the Crays. Although well established as a force in senior football, the club has been in "exile" since vacating the Grassmeade ground in 1972. Since then, the club has played outside the Crays - at Oxford Road in Sidcup, and then at Hayes Lane the home of Bromley FC.

"Football's Coming Home!" That is the mission statement of Cray Wanderers in its 150th anniversary year. We have announced a plan to build a new stadium in Sandy Lane, St Paul's Cray. This will bring Cray Wanderers back to the club's true home, in the heartland of the Crays.'

**Cray Wanderers FC
1860 -2010**

Gary Hillman and everyone in the Cray Wanderers club must have been heartened to see such a big turn-out of supporters at the game. An attendance of nearly 500 signified that the Cray Wanderers still very much belongs to the Crays.

Two goals by Danny Phillips and one from Shane Graham saw the Wands run out 3-0 winners of a hard-fought game.

**Cray Wanderers FC
1860 -2010**

Right: Sarah Hodson
models the new "1860
Retro" shirt, with Cray
players Mark Willy and
Danny Phillips.
Photo: Trevor Mulligan.

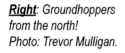

Right: Groundhoppers
from the north!
Photo: Trevor Mulligan.

Far Right: Gary Hillman
welcomes Jo Johnson,
MP for Orpington, to the
game.
Photo: Trevor Mulligan.

Cray Wanderers FC
1860 -2010

Next up in the exciting calendar of 'Cray 150' special events during the summer of 2010 was a friendly match on 14 July versus Leyton Orient of the Npower Division One.

The O's kindly brought their full first team squad for this fixture, thereby marking the first-ever time in 150 years that Cray Wanderers had played against Football League strength opponents.

The fixture had been organised a few weeks earlier, after the O's had swooped to sign Cray's young prodigy George Porter at the end of the 2009-10 season. George signed a two-year professional contract at Brisbane Road.

From the first moment that George moved up from Cray's academy team to make his first team debut for the Wands at AF.C. Hornchurch in September 2009, it looked certain that he was destined to go much higher in the game. He just got better and better – and even some of the best and most experienced Ryman Premier defenders couldn't cope with him.

The Cray v Leyton Orient friendly match on 14 July attracted an attendance of 325, with the visitors gaining a tight-fought 2-0 win. Ironically, the opening goal came from a penalty-kick that was awarded against Cray for a foul on their former young player!

George made his full first team debut for the O's when he came on as substitute after 71 minutes versus Charlton Athletic in a Division One match on 13 August 2010. This made George the first-ever player in Cray Wanderers history to go straight into the Football League, from Cray.

Everyone at Cray Wanderers will wish George the very best for his future. We will be keeping a keen eye on his progress, that's for sure.

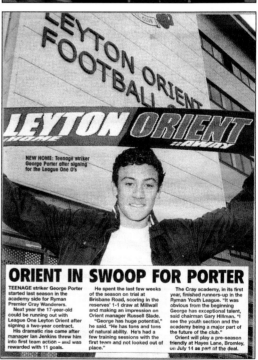

NEW HOME: Teenage striker George Porter after signing for the League One O's

ORIENT IN SWOOP FOR PORTER

TEENAGE striker George Porter started last season in the academy side for Ryman Premier Cray Wanderers.

Next year the 17-year-old could be running out with League One Leyton Orient after signing a two-year contract.

His dramatic rise came after manager Ian Jenkins threw him into first team action – and was rewarded with 11 goals.

He spent the last few weeks of the season on trial at Brisbane Road, scoring in the reserves' 1-1 draw at Millwall and making an impression on Orient manager Russell Slade.

"George has huge potential," he said. "He has tons and tons of natural ability. He's had a few training sessions with the first team and not looked out of place."

The Cray academy, in its first year, finished runners-up in the Ryman Youth League. "It was obvious from the beginning George has exceptional talent, said chairman Gary Hillman. "I see the youth section and the academy being a major part of the future of the club."

Orient will play a pre-season friendly at Hayes Lane, Bromley, on July 14 as part of the deal.

Cray Wanderers FC
1860 -2010

Chapter13 - The Heritage Tournament at Sheffield FC

When the club historians look back and tally up some of the best 'Cray Days' that there have ever been, they will surely have to include the 31 July 2010 when the Wands took part in and won the Heritage Tournament, at Sheffield FC.

This unique event in world football history was a one-day round-robin tournament featuring the three oldest football clubs: Sheffield F.C. (1857), Cray Wanderers F.C. (1860) and Hallam F.C. (1860).

The three teams played each other in sixty-minute matches kicking off at 1pm, 2.30pm and 4pm.

First was the all-Yorkshire derby, with Hallam beating Sheffield 1-0.

Cray then took the field and defeated Hallam 1-0 thanks to a last-minute headed goal by Ola Smith.

Continuing with the fast and fluent passing style of football that had earned them plenty of praise from the spectators during the Hallam game, the Wands dominated the first half versus Sheffield and took the lead through Richard Whyte's header.

Tiring in the second half, the Wands conceded two late goals and it ended 2-1 to Sheffield.

The rules held that Cray and Sheffield, the joint top-scoring teams, had to go into a sudden-death penalty shoot-out to decide the winners of the Heritage Tournament.

The tension was becoming unbearable when the score reached 6-6 with no one having missed from the spot.

Up stepped Fraser Cronin, the youngest member of the Cray squad, and he coolly chipped in the spot-kick to seal victory for the Wands by 7-6.

The Wands were obviously elated to have won this special tournament (described by chairman Gary Hillman as "winning the World Cup"!).

It was above all a great sporting occasion, and a true celebration of football. We must congratulate Sheffield F.C. for their admirable organisation of the event.

Cray Wanderers FC
1860 -2010

**Cray Wanderers FC
1860 -2010**

Chapter 14 Cray Wanderers v Guyana All Stars International Team, 8 August 2010

**Cray Wanderers FC
1860 -2010**

Cray Wanderers playing against an international team?

Imagine what the St Mary Cray villagers of 1860 would have thought of that?

But sure enough, at Dulwich Hamlet F.C. on the 8 August 2010, Cray Wanderers marked another amazing "first" in their long history when they stepped out to play Guyana in a specially-arranged international friendly match.

It was a big day for Guyana and their many supporters too, for it was the first ever time that the Guyanese full international side had played a match in Britain.

The spectators were entertained by a thrilling and fast-flowing game that ended 1-1.

John Guest headed Cray into the lead after 4 minutes, but after strong pressure in the second half, Guyana deservedly levelled the score in the 90th minute.

Extra time could not separate the teams, and so for the second time in eight days the Wands found themselves going into a penalty shoot-out.

And it was the Wands who held their nerve to win on penalties 4-3, despite the best efforts of Guyana's substitute goalkeeper Jason Lloyd whose famous cricketing father Clive Lloyd was watching the game.

Highlights of the game were televised on Sky Sports One's FIFA Futbol Mondial on 1st September. Another first for the Wands!

Cray Wanderers FC
1860 -2010

Cray Wanderers FC
1860 -2010

Saturday, February 2nd, 1929

CRAY WANDERERS
Amber and Black Jerseys.

Goal.
1
H. Hart.

Backs.

2
F. Terry,

3
S. A. Gilbey.

Half-backs.

4
T. Banks.

5
R. Coleman (Vice-Capt.)

6
G. A. Miles,

Forwards.

7
A. E. Rose,

8
A. N. Chevis,

10
H. Jones,

11
J. Davies.

9
C. Tomlinson.

Referee—Mr. J. C. BATTISON (Leigh-on-Sea.)

L. Grainger.
14.

W. Padbury,
12.

A. Baker,
13.

R. Sargeant,
15.

H. E. Watson.
16.

Forwards.

J. Newton,
17.

B. J. Dadley,
18.

F. Finch.
19.

Half-backs.

W. Samuel,
20.

R. Cook.
21.

Backs.

H. Handley.
22.

Goal.

CARSHALTON

Beyond stating that our boys fully deserved their win over Bromley last week, I do not propose to remark on the match.

There is no doubt that many did not realise the gravity of the injury which our Captain (Mr. S. R. Ware) sustained last Saturday. Immediately after the match, medical evidence was sought and Mr. Ware was subsequently ordered to the Cray Valley Hospital for X-Ray examination which, I regret to say, revealed that he had sustained a fracture of the Pelvis. The injury will result in his total incapacity for at least six weeks, although if he progresses satisfactorily there is a possibility of his starting light work after a similar period of convalescence. Mr. Ware has decided to retire from the game but even if this were not his intention, it would be a physical impossibility for him to play again until eighteen months hence.

Thus has this Club sustained an almost irreparable loss in most tragic circumstances. In Mr. Ware we have lost not only a pal, worthy of the name, but, also a valued playing member who, by his play, enthusiasm and many other splendid qualities, has been largely instrumental in raising this Club to its present position. His conduct, both on and off the Field, will, I am sure, be remembered as symbolical of all that which is best in a thoroughly sportsman and gentleman.

We can only wish him a speedy and successful recovery for at this juncture we can do nothing to help him. If, however, a trainer or two can offer him help, then it must be the pleasure and privilege of both Management and supporters, in their personal capacities, to prove that our regard for him has been, and still is, sincere, and so demonstrate to him that his faith in us, and the Cause we represent, has not been misplaced.

Next week we visit A.P.C.M. in the Kent Amateur Cup. The Ground is 1½ miles from Aylesford Station. H.H.O.

G. P. HARLAND, 11, POPLAR TERRACE, (our Trainer), is open for engagements at Dances, Public or Private, with his new up-to-date Drum Set.

No. 291

C·W F·C

FOUNDED 1860   Hon. Sec. M. P. SLATER

CRAY WANDERERS

Members of the London League   Affiliated to K.C.F.A.

FOUNDED 1860   Hon. Sec. — M. P. SLATER

C·W·F·C

Members of the London League   Affiliated to K.C.F.A.

CRAY WANDERERS

VERSUS Nº 577

BRENTSTONIANS
KICK OFF 2.45 p.m.
SATURDAY 23rd, JANUARY, 1954
FORDCROFT, ST. MARY CRAY

Next home game ETON MANOR 3 p.m.

Patron . . Sir Waldron Smithers, J.P., M.P.

VERSUS

London League
ETON MANOR
Saturday, 11th February 1956
Grassmeade . . St. Mary Cray
K.O. 3.0 p.m.

President :   Colours:
Donald Sumner, O.B.E., M.P.   Black and Amber   *Programme 3d*

**Cray Wanderers FC
1860 -2010**

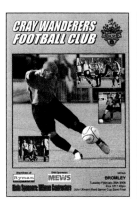

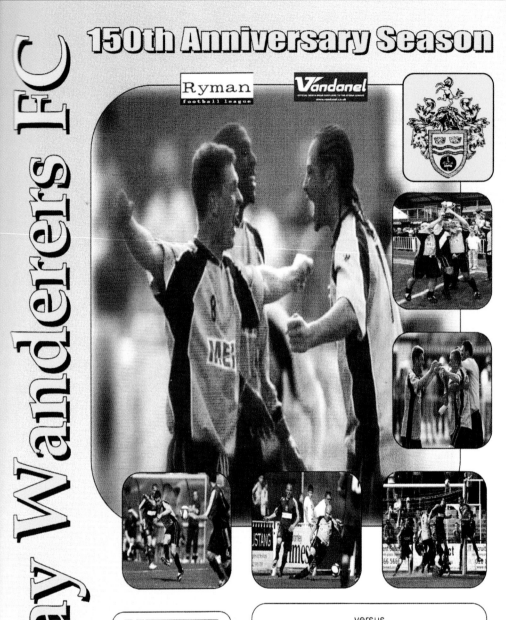

150th Anniversary Season

Ryman
football league

Vandanel

HILLMAN
EST 1958
www.craywands.co.uk

versus
CARSHALTON ATHLETIC
Sunday October 25th 2009 (3.00pm)
Ryman League Premier Division

Official Match Day Programme - £2.00

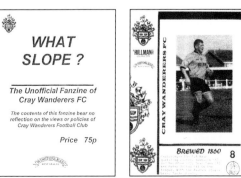

WHAT
SLOPE ?

The Unofficial Fanzine of
Cray Wanderers FC

The contents of this fanzine bear no
reflection on the views or policies of
Cray Wanderers Football Club

Price   75p

Chapter 16 Cray Wanderers Away Programmes

Cray Wanderers FC
1860 -2010

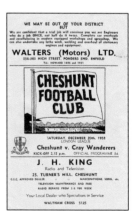

1922 Catford Southend
1929 Bromley
1929 Chelmsford
1931 Aylesford PM
1932 Park Royal
1936 Bexleyheath &
     Welling
1949 Churchfields OB
1948 Churchfields OB
1953 Floodlight Football
1957 Aveley
1958 Barkingside
1958 Cheshunt
1958 East HamUnited
1958 Maidstone United
1958 Redhill
1958 Sheppey United

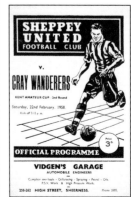

Cray Wanderers FC
1860 -2010

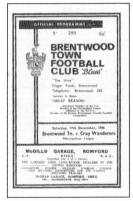

1958 Wingate
1963 Barnet
1963 Herne Bay
1964 Dartford
1964 KAC final
1965 Canterbury City
1966 Brentwood
1966 Erith & Belvedere
1966 Harlow Town
1969 Leytonstone
1969 Wellingborough
Town
1971 Bletchley
1973 Hampton
1974 Walton & Hersham
1979 Kingstonian
1979 Chatham Town

**Cray Wanderers FC
1860 -2010**

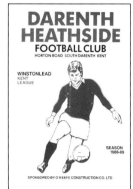

1981 Great Yarmouth
1984 Thorn EMI
1985 4 Area Met Police
1988 Darenth Heathside
1990 Tonbridge
1992 Alma Swanley
1993 Dartford FC
1993 Furness
1993 KST Final
1996 Beckenham Town
1996 Ford United
1996 Thamesmead Town
1996 Whitstable Town
1997 Corinthian
1997 Wingate & Finchley
1998 Crockenhill

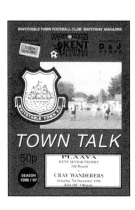

**Cray Wanderers FC
1860 -2010**

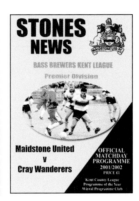

Chapter 17 Miscellaneous items

**Cray Wanderers FC
1860 -2010**

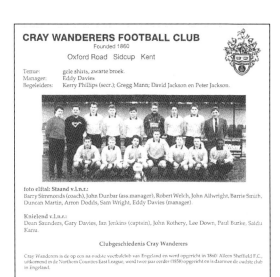

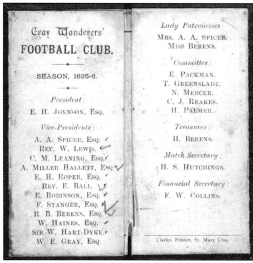

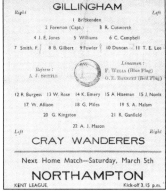

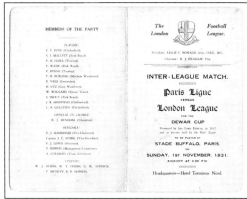

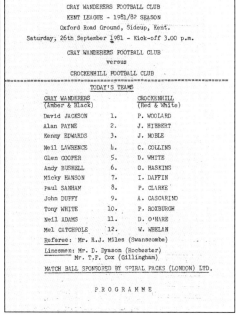

**Cray Wanderers FC
1860 -2010**

**Cray Wanderers FC
1860 -2010**

Cray Wanderers FC
1860 -2010

Founded 1860

**Cray Wanderers FC
1860 -2010**

Cray Wanderers FC
1860 -2010

Gallery images: We took a decision not to caption any of the photos in this section as so many names would be needed. We trust that all those who feature in the images are proud to be part of this book. We defy anyone to be able to name everyone featured - we couldn't!

Chapter 18 Thanks

**Cray Wanderers FC
1860 -2010**

Well, that is our summary of the first 150 years' history of Cray Wanderers Football Club. We hope that you have found it to be an interesting and enjoyable read. We trust that there will be plenty more exciting and successful exploits in the future, to fill the Wands' history books at the 200th, 250th and 300th anniversaries, and on into the future!

Perhaps the current season 2010-11 will feature as one of the best and most memorable ones in the club's history. It has already brought plenty of excitement during the opening weeks. Laurent Hamici, a new (French-born) striker has raced into double figures inside the first two months of the season, netting two hat-tricks in September alone. On the FA Cup trail the Wands have been visited and filmed by ITV Sport – a fitting choice, we might say, in view of the Wands being in the spotlight this year with their 150th anniversary.

Thank You

When attempting to thank everyone who has kindly assisted us in putting together this book we have an almost impossible task. We can say only that we express our gratitude to every single person who has kindly helped us by providing information, memories, old photos and programmes, and goodwill.

We provide hereunder a short biography of Mike, Jerry and Peter who have edited and written the book. Extra special thanks must go to Ian Fordyce for his valuable input on the club history and statistics, and his many memories of the club - he has supported the Wands since the 1950s. We must likewise thank Kevin Goodhew for all his work during the 1980s when we started trying to compile a detailed history and photographic record of the club. To long-term sup-

porter and current webmaster Trevor Mulligan we say a grateful thank you for his numerous contributions. We thank too Melody Foreman (Group Editor, *Kentish Times* Newspapers) and Paul Green (Sports Editor, *News Shopper*) for their kind permission to use published material from their newspaper archives.

Jerry Dowlen (Co-author)

Jerry began watching Cray Wanderers in 1959. He has served on the club committee since 1994. Jerry started up the much-admired *Cray Chatter* magazine (some would call it a Fanzine) that ran to more than 70 issues between 1980 ans 2002. It was instrumental in starting to piece together the club history, capturing precious information and memories from many old players and supporters going back to village times in St Mary Cray.

Jerry has published individual books on Ken Collishaw (his all-time favourite Cray player) and on Cray supporter Donald 'Ted' Ward, poet and pacifist.

Peter Goringe (Co-author)

Peter tells us that his first Cray game was v Ulysses in May 1975 (3-0); best goal was Ross Lover's at Waltham Forest in the F.A. Trophy in 2006 ('that' volley!); best game was the 4-3 KLC final v Sheppey at Sittingbourne in 1984 (although the most memorable was the 2-0 win versus Lordswood to win the Kent League in 2003.). Peter is not sure that he has an all-time favourite Cray player but, if pushed, would say Butch Dunn, with Phil Williams a close second. After moving away from Sidcup to pursue his career in education and to bring up a family in Needham Market, Banbury and now Kettering, Peter has continued to

follow the Wands very closely from a distance, and has rendered the club good service with his tireless work on the club history, statistics (past and present) and his numerous written contributions to the match programme and other club publications.

Mike Floate (Editor)

Peter Goringe writes: Born in Beckenham but having lived in Swansea for many years Mike has followed Swansea City at away games from Exeter to Newcastle. Mike is known throughout the world of Non-League football for his association with Crockenhill F.C., who were for many years the Wands' closest rivals. He is acknowledged as a leading authority on football grounds. His first booklet on grounds in Kent appeared back in the mid-1990s and he has since, through his own company, Newlands Publishing, produced the hugely-respected 'The Non-League Grounds of....' series, which has set new standards for the quality of its meticulous research and photography. A range of other publications, frequent magazine articles and a lively website have made Mike a household name amongst hard-core enthusiasts of grassroots football.

Mike adds: I moved back to London in 1980 and decided to see what local football had to offer. One of the first games I saw was the F.A. Vase Quarter Final tie against Stamford. The atmosphere at Oxford Road was so good that I decided to watch Cray in further cup ties, including the memorable game at Sittingbourne already mentioned by Peter Goringe.
Jerry Dowlen's *Cray Chatter* had a big effect on me, with one issue sending me searching for

Catford South-end's ground which was probably the start of my interest in uncovering the history of local grounds. By this time I was also taking action photos and was a contributor to *Team Talk* and the *Non-League*

Directory. As no fees were payable the chance to be paid to write illustrated features for the rival *Non-League Football Today* magazine was a natural progression. The closure of the magazine took me to Crockenhill, my local club. I had first visited the delightful Wested Meadow ground with Cray for an F.A. Vase tie in 1983 and this led me to move to the village.

I am delighted to read Peter's comments on my books. With the series now running to fifteen titles the most recent editions have been full colour paperbacks, a long way from the spiral bound and photocopied booklets of 1995.

Details of the titles available are listed below. To buy please send a cheque to me at Newlands Cottages, Stones Cross Road, Crockenhill, Swanley, Kent BR8 8LT. My Football Grounds Frenzy website has pages with paypal links for online purchases. All purchases are post free.

Non-League Grounds of Liverpool & Manchester *by T Gorman* £14.95; Non-League Grounds of Lancashire *by T Gorman* £17.95; Football Grounds of South East London *by M Floate* £12.95; Non-League Grounds of Cheshire *by J Keohane* £9.95; Football Grounds of Rural Essex *by J Weaver* £11.95; Football Grounds of Essex Metropolitan *by J Weaver* £9.95; Lost Grounds of Essex *by J Weaver* £14.95; Non-League Grounds of Staffs & Shropshire *by C Peel & M Blakeman* £9.95; Non-League Grounds of Sussex *by D Bauckham* £9.95; Non-League Grounds of West Yorkshire *by S Mumford* £6.95;

Photographs

The vast majority of images have come from club archives. Whenever possible we have tried to credit individual photographers for their work, but this became difficult in certain chapters.

Images in Chapters 4 & 5 by Jerry Dowlen, Kevin Goodhew, Steve Hodson, Neil Howick, Ollie Musgrove, Andy Nunn and Simon Roe. Uncredited images in Chapters 12 - 15 by Simon Roe. Back cover: top two images by Alan Coombs.

We would wish to thank the above photographers and those credited through the book for the use of their work which has made an interesting story become more real and personal.